THE OBSERVER'S DIRECTORY OF
BRITISH STEAM LOCOMOTIVES

The Observer's Directory of

BRITISH STEAM
LOCOMOTIVES

H. C. Casserley

FREDERICK WARNE

Published by
Frederick Warne (Publishers) Ltd, London 1980
© Frederick Warne (Publishers) Ltd 1980

ISBN 0 7232 2413 7

Phototypeset by Tradespools Ltd, Frome, Somerset
Printed in Great Britain by
Butler and Tanner Ltd, Frome and London

CONTENTS

Acknowledgements

Thanks are given to the following copyright owners and photographers for their kind permission to reproduce photographs in this book:

Ian Allan Ltd for photographs 25, 47, 151, 186, 235, 416, 422, 427, 460, 526, 541, 558 formerly belonging to the Locomotive Publishing Co Ltd and 57, 100, 110, 305, 356, 364, 480 by O. J. Morris; R. J. Buckley for 51, 62, 82, 101, 149, 302, 321, 322, 325, 375, 396, 407, 455, 458, 466, 475, 476; W. Clark for 388; A. F. Cook for 474; T. G. Hepburn for 236; R. Higgins for 531; K. A. Jaggers for 18; F. Jones for 67; G. D. King for 326; L. B. Lapper for 535; L. C. G. B. Ken Nunn Collection for 123, 494; Photomatic for 414, 428, 495, 557, 559; R. C. Riley for 544; P. B. Whitehouse for 22. Photographs 32, 124, 145, 156, 210, 514 by L & GRP are by courtesy of David & Charles. Drawings 9, 46 and 265 are by Ray Martin.

The majority of other photographs were taken by the author. In a few cases it has been impossible to trace the owners and we apologize for the infringement of any copyright.

Foreword

This directory of British steam locomotives is presented in a novel form which will, it is hoped, highlight new aspects of their fascinating history. The main section comprises a survey based on wheel arrangement, one of the fundamentals of locomotive design. Within each section, the individual engines are described in chronological order, demonstrating the development of the type. The pictures are chosen to portray a wide range of periods where such a selection is possible. In the case of older and long lived classes, some may be shown in their early or pre-1923 condition, others as running during the period of the grouping from 1923 to 1947, and a few in their last years after nationalisation to give a general picture of the changing styles over the years.

The illustrations, many of which are of a historic nature, have been obtained from a variety of sources, and a number are of unknown origin. In order that as many locomotives as possible are illustrated, the photographs have, where necessary, been supplemented by sketches.

Principal dimensions are given for each class, together with a short history. From the 'observer's' point of view, special attention has been paid to such examples as have fortunately survived, and which can be seen today in museums, preservation centres and on working railways. A list of these is given at the back of the book.

THE EARLY YEARS 1804–54

1 The history of the steam locomotive running on rails goes back to the year 1804, when Richard Trevithick constructed an engine for use on the tramway at Pen-y-Darren ironworks at Merthyr Tydfil in South Wales. Steam driven road vehicles, of a sort, had already appeared during the later years of the 18th century, some indeed actually the work of Trevithick, but they do not come within the scope of this review.

Such details of this pioneer railway engine which have survived are somewhat incomplete. Even its actual appearance can only be a matter of conjecture from such meagre evidence of the time which can be traced. It has however been possible to construct a model, to be seen in the Science Museum, Kensington, which no doubt bears a fairly accurate resemblance to the original.

The only dimensions recorded are that it had 3ft 9in driving wheels, and that the single cylinder was of 8in bore and 4ft 6in stroke. The locomotive weighed approximately five tons. It will be seen from the illustration that this machine bore little resemblance to the modern locomotive, the genesis of which was not to appear for another three decades. For one thing, its boiler had only a single return flue traversing the barrel once in either direction. The multi-tubular boiler, one of the most important features of standard locomotive design, which was to last right until the end of steam, did not appear until 1829 on Stephenson's *Rocket*. On the Pen-y-Darren loco a large flywheel was necessary to keep the engine in motion at the end of each cycle of operation of the single cylinder. This feature became unnecessary with the

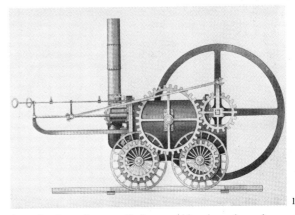

1

introduction of two cylinders working in unison; however, it survived until recent years on single-cylinder steam traction engines and steam rollers.

During the following couple of decades of gradual modification and improvement the standard features of future locomotive design were developed. They included the multitubular boiler and the blast pipe, which forced exhaust steam from the cylinders up the chimney. These innovations resulted in the unique characteristic of the conventional steam locomotive: the harder the engine is worked the more energy is automatically produced by the creation of a fiercer fire and the production of more steam. It is fairly certain that in the Pen-y-Darren loco the exhaust steam was passed up into the chimney, but only as a means of getting rid of it; Trevithick was not aware of the beneficial effects at the time, and he took out no patent for its application.

As early as 1812 an engine was built by one Matthew Murray to the order of John Blenkinsop, of the Middleton Colliery, Leeds. This is incidentally the oldest railway still in existence, dating back to 1758. The engine was unusual in that it had a toothed driving wheel engaging a rack rail alongside the normal running rails. Blenkinsop did not believe there would be sufficient adhesion between smooth wheels and rail for normal working. This theory was of course soon entirely discounted. Such a device is however still used on mountain railways with gradients of 1 in 5 or so, for example the Snowdon Mountain Railway (see **86**).

Wylam Dilly, the oldest engine still in existence, was built in 1813 by William Hedley, assistant to Timothy Hackworth. Its 3ft 3in driving wheels, four coupled, were connected through a train of spur wheels to a central driving crankshaft. Its cylinders were 9 × 36in, working pressure was 50lb per square inch, and the engine, without tender, weighed eight tons.

The engine can be seen in the Royal Scottish Museum, Edinburgh.

Almost contemporary with *Wylam Dilly* and of very similar appearance, *Puffing Billy* was also built by Hedley in 1814. It may now be seen in South Kensington Museum.

2 The Hetton Colliery engine of 1822, now to be seen at the Beamish Museum, Durham, was the work of George Stephenson. It appeared in the procession (though not under steam) at the Darlington Centenary of 1925.

2

By this time it was found possible to use a boiler pressure of 80lb per square inch. This allowed the cylinder dimensions to be reduced to 10¼ × 24in, approaching the proportions which were to become usual in the future.

3 *Locomotion No 1* was built by Stephenson for the newly opened Stockton & Darlington Railway in 1825. The original engine was for many years mounted on a plinth at Darlington main station, and is now preserved at the small BR museum at Darlington North Road. A full-sized working replica is also in existence, built to take part in the 1975 celebrations at Shildon, marking the 150th anniversary of the opening of the railway.

3

5

4

4 Stephenson's *Rocket* of 1829 was originally constructed with the cylinders sloped at an angle of 45 degrees. A working replica has been built to take part in the Liverpool & Manchester 150th anniversary at Rainhill in 1980.

The original locomotive was later rebuilt with almost horizontal cylinders and modifications to the smokebox. This modified locomotive is now to be seen in the Science Museum, South Kensington.

5 Timothy Hackworth's entry for the Rainhill trials of 1829, of which Stephenson's *Rocket* was the winner, was an 0-4-0, *Sanspareil*. In the event it was excluded because its weight exceeded the permitted maximum. It now rests in South Kensington Museum together with the *Rocket* itself.

Another contestant in the Rainhill trials was the curious vertical-boilered engine *Novelty*, built by Braithwaite & Ericsson in 1829. It had 4ft 2in driving wheels, the upright cylinders were 6 × 12in and it weighed 2¾ tons. Parts of it are still in existence, although not on public view, but it is proposed at the time of writing to build a working replica for use in the Rainhill celebrations commemorating the 150th anniversary of the Liverpool & Manchester Railway.

6 *Invicta* was built for the Canterbury & Whitstable Railway in 1830. It worked on this line until about 1839. For many years it has been on exhibition in Canterbury Gardens, but at the time of writing it is undergoing renovation at the NRM premises at York.

7 *Billy* was built in 1830 by the firm of Robert Stephenson & Co. of Newcastle on Tyne. This, the first locomotive works in the world, was founded in 1823 by George Stephenson and his son Robert, who followed in his father's footsteps as a railway engineer. *Billy* was built for

7

the Killingworth Colliery railway, on which it ran until 1881. It is now in Newcastle Municipal Museum.

8 *Hibernia*, the first engine in Ireland, was built by Sharp Roberts in 1834 for the Dublin & Kingston Railway. It will be noted that the 11 × 16in cylinders still retained the vertical position, the piston and connecting rods being joined by a heavy triangular bell crank. It had 5ft 0in driving wheels.

9 In 1830 Stephenson's *Planet* appeared, a small primitive 2-2-0 which combined the basic essentials of the modern steam locomotive: multitubular boiler with cylinder exhaust up the chimney, horizontal cylinders placed beneath the smokebox instead of vertical or steeply angled ones, and the steam engine itself mounted on independent framing. Previously the boiler had been the main framework of the engine, on to which cylinders and other accessories were mounted.

6

8

9

firebox; all early improvements. These were to be followed in due course by advances in the design of valve gear and the more economical use of steam through such devices as compounding, superheating and multiple blast pipes.

10 A natural development of the primitive 2-2-0 was Stephenson's *Patentee* of 1833. It was built for the Liverpool & Manchester, and was the forerunner of many similar designs produced during the ensuing years.

10

This design was the basis for the many technical improvements which were to follow in future years. These included such advances as the invention of injectors in place of feed pumps to replenish the water supply to the boiler, steam and vacuum brakes supplementing the more primitive handbrakes, and the brick arch in the

11 The Jenny Lind class was designed by David Joy for the Midland Railway and built by E. B. Wilson & Co. from 1847 onwards. It was typical of the engines inspired by *Patentee*. They had 6ft 0in driving wheels and 15 × 20in cylinders. The boiler pressure of 120lb per square inch, possibly the highest used up to that time, probably accounted for the great success of these engines.

11

12

12 A fortunate survival of early years is *Lion*, an 0-4-2 of the Liverpool & Manchester Railway built by Todd Kitson & Laird in 1838. On withdrawal from active service in 1859 it was purchased by the Mersey Docks & Harbour Board for use as a stationary boiler. In this humble capacity it worked for many years, unknown to the railway world at large.

In the 1920s it was brought to the notice of the LMS who purchased it and restored it to working order. Since then it has been in steam on various occasions and more than once has been hired by film companies for appearance in early railway scenes. It was brought to Euston in September 1938 for the London & Birmingham Railway centenary, as seen in the photograph. It is now in Liverpool Museum. Note the 'haystack' firebox, more usually found on Bury engines (see **16**).

13 A number of 4-2-0s were imported from America between 1839 and 1841 for use on the Birmingham & Gloucester Railway (later part of the Midland system). Some were intended specially for use as bankers on the famous Lickey Incline, with a continuous ascent of over two miles with a gradient of 1 in 37. They were a very early example of engines being imported from abroad for use in Britain, although British builders have constructed many thousands of locomotives for use all over the world.

These engines were designed by William Norris of Philadelphia, but some were built in England to his design. The last survivors disappeared in 1856. The driving wheels were 4ft 0in in diameter, and 10½ × 18in cylinders were employed.

14 *North Star*, one of the earliest and best known of the GWR's 7ft 0in broad gauge engines, was built by R. Stephenson & Co. in 1837. On withdrawal in 1871 it was preserved at Swindon, to be joined later by one of the larger 4-2-2s, *Lord of the Isles*. Unfortunately, and almost

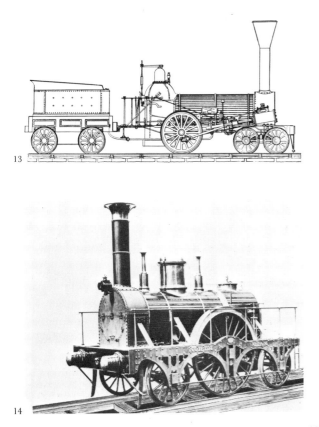

13

14

incredibly in this more preservation conscious age, they were broken up in 1906. The wheels of *North Star* somehow survived, and were incorporated into a new full-sized replica built in 1925 for the Darlington Centenary, and it is this reconstruction which can today be seen in Swindon Museum. Its driving wheels are 7ft 0in in diameter, cylinders 16 × 16in and it weighs 23 tons 7 cwt.

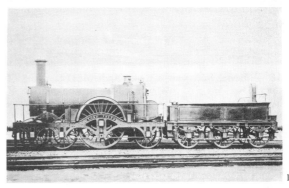

15

15 *Lord of the Isles* was a 4-2-2 of the Iron Duke class, which comprised 29 engines in all built between 1847 and 1855. They worked the principal expresses right through to the abolition of the broad gauge in 1892. The engines were then pensioned off, despite the fact that 24 of them had been considerably renewed so as to be virtually new engines, although identical with the original design. Like *North Star*, *Lord of the Isles* was ruthlessly consigned to the scrap heap in 1906.

21 Another early LNWR survival, *Cornwall*, was built in 1847 as a 2-2-2 with 8ft 6in drivers by Francis Trevithick. Its boiler was underslung below the driving axle, the idea apparently being to obtain a low centre of gravity.

For a time the engine ran as a 4-2-2, but the experiment does not seem to have been a success as it was rebuilt by Ramsbottom in 1858 on more conventional lines, and it will be seen that it acquired the Allan type of smokebox and framing. In this form *Cornwall* had a long life and finished up working the directors' saloon until as late as 1927. It is now preserved at Crewe (**22**).

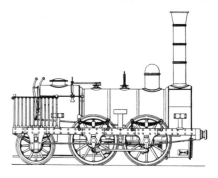

23

21

22

23 As the 2-2-2 was a natural development for passenger work of the 2-2-0, so the 0-4-0 type developed into the 0-4-2 for goods traffic and in turn to the 0-6-0, although the 0-4-2 remained a favourite on several railways for many years. The first inside-cylinder engines of both wheel arrangements, all built by R. Stephenson & Co., were two 0-4-2s in 1833 for the Leicester & Swannington Railway, genesis of the Midland Railway. These were followed by others in 1834 for the Stanhope & Tyne Railway.

In the same year, some 0-6-0s were built for the Leicester & Swannington Railway. These had 4ft 6in driving wheels with 16 × 20in cylinders, a considerable advance on the 14 × 18in of the 0-4-2s. The normal boiler pressure of that period was around 50lb. As a point of minor interest the L&S 0-4-2s are believed to have been the first engines to have been fitted with a steam whistle, a sound eventually to recall so many nostalgic memories.

24 Thomas Russell Crampton was another highly individual designer, the main feature of his engines being a large pair of single driving wheels situated at the rear and behind the firebox, together with such forward carrying wheels as were found necessary. Most had outside cylinders, but an inside-cylinder version was also produced, needing a dummy crankshaft in front of the firebox, and the design appeared on a number of railways, such as the LNER, Midland, and South Eastern Railways. One of the latter, No 136 *Folkestone*, built by R. Stephenson & Co. in 1851, was exhibited at the Exhibition in Hyde Park in that year. It gives a general idea of the appearance of these somewhat extraordinary machines. They were particularly popular on the Continent, and one is to be found preserved in the French National Collection at Mulhouse. No example has survived in this country. There were many varieties of them, but the SER engine had 6ft 0in driving wheels and 15 × 22in cylinders, and it weighed 26¼ tons.

25 Apart from the Norris 4-2-0s of the Birmingham & Gloucester Railway (see **13**), Sturrock's 4-2-2 of 1853 for the Great Northern seems to have been the first engine to be fitted with a swivelling front bogie. (In the GWR broad gauge Iron Duke class, the leading wheels were rigid with the main framing.) It had 7ft 6in driving wheels and 17 × 24in cylinders. The long wheelbase of the independent bogie measured 7ft 2in. It was a large locomotive for its day, but only one of the class was built. It ran until 1870.

PRINCIPAL LOCOMOTIVE DESIGNS, 1855–1954

This second and main part of the history of the British steam locomotive covers the period of 100 years from 1855, by which time progress in design had passed the initial experimental stage and had settled down to a process of continuous improvement, development, and of course enlargement right up to the year 1954. This was the fatal year when the last new design came off the drawing boards and henceforth a gradual – not too gradual as it turned out – change over to diesel and electric propulsion would be the policy of the future.

The story of this progress and development has been written in various forms many times before, but the plan which has been devised for this treatise is one which it is thought has never previously been followed. It is hoped that it will provide a unique angle from which to study the various changes, innovations and improvements which have taken place over the years.

Briefly, the scheme is based on the wheel arrangements which have been employed, a very important consideration in design depending on the duties for which the locomotives are intended. Early engines usually had four or six wheels, of which one pair would be the actual drivers, and the others the carrying wheels. As the engines grew larger the number of wheels increased and coupled driving wheels were introduced to give greater rail adhesion.

The various wheel arrangements were eventually classified into what came to be known as the Whyte notation. The figures denoted respectively the number of leading idle wheels, then the driving wheels, and finally the trailing idle wheels, if any. Thus a plain express engine of the early days could be a 2-2-2, with a single pair of large drivers for speed. A freight locomotive, usually with smaller driving wheels to favour power rather than speed, had all its axles coupled to minimise wheelspin, often in the form of a 0-4-0 or 0-6-0. The largest express design to be commonly employed in Britain was the 4-6-2 (generally known as a Pacific, from its usual designation in America). The largest freight design was for many years the 2-8-0, and ultimately the 2-10-0.

Main line engines carried their fuel supplies in a separate unit, the tender. This was normally of six wheels, but occasionally eight; these wheels were not included in the Whyte notation. Engines for short distance work and shunting duties however carried their coal and water supplies aboard. The water was usually contained in tanks situated on either side of the boiler, in which case the Whyte formula would read 0-4-4T or whatever. Sometimes the tank took the form of a saddle mounted on the boiler, resulting in a designation such as 0-6-0ST. Occasionally the water was carried in two separate tanks, also mounted actually on the boiler and not on the engine framing as in the case of side tanks. These were described as pannier tanks, for example 0-6-0PT. Other engines carried their water supplies in tanks out of sight beneath the coal bunker; these were well tanks with the designation WT.

In this book various locomotives are examined in order of the number of driving wheels, starting with the 2-2-2 arrangement, and continuing through to the 2-10-0. The tender engines in each group are followed by the tank classes.

A few 'out of the run' wheel arrangements, such as the Garratt and other designs, which do not readily conform to the Whyte notation, are dealt with on pages 211–17.

2-2-2

Several early 2-2-2s have already received attention in the first section dealing with the period up to 1854. The type, however, continued to be built alongside progressively larger designs right through to the final years of the nineteenth century.

26 Ramsbottom's Lady of the Lake class (sometimes known as Problems) of which there were 60 in all, came out between 1859 and 1865, and were long-lived engines. They were all rebuilt by Mr Webb between 1895 and 1899, with boiler pressure increased from 120lb to 150lb per square inch, giving them several more years of useful life. The last of them were taken out of traffic in 1907. They had 7ft 7½in driving wheels and 16 × 24in cylinders.

27

27 Matthew Kirtley built 74 2-2-2s with double frames for the Midland Railway from the late 1850s until 1866. Most of them were rebuilt by Johnson, and like their LNWR counterparts, some lasted beyond the turn of the century, two until 1905. No more single-wheelers were built for the Midland until the famous Johnson 4-2-2s in 1887 (see **37**).

No 39 was built at Derby in 1864 and worked until 1895. It had 6ft 8½in driving wheels and 16½ × 22in cylinders.

28 Between 1874 and 1882 William Stroudley built 26 very pretty little 2-2-2s for the LB&SCR, several years after its neighbours, the LSWR, SER, and LC&DR had abandoned construction of single-wheelers. The South Western indeed built no more for express work after 1859, discounting Drummond's double single 4-(2-2)-0 engines.

The Brighton engines did very fine work on the LB&SCR main lines right into the Edwardian era. Scrapping did not begin until 1907, and No 329 *Stephenson*, by that time 329A, was even entrusted with regularly

26

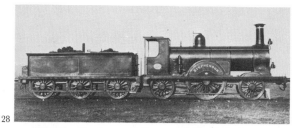

28

working the *Eastbourne Pullman*, a fairly light but nevertheless important train, as late as 1910. It was not finally broken up until 1914.

These remarkable little engines had 6ft 6in driving wheels and 17 × 24in cylinders. They had a working pressure of 140lb, later raised to 150lb.

29 Another railway which employed 2-2-2 engines on top link duties until a comparatively late period was the Great Northern. Between 1885 and 1894 Patrick Stirling built 23 new engines which were virtually identical with a much earlier design of 1868, but with increased dimensions. These worked alongside his better known 8ft 0in 4-2-2s (see **35**) on the principal express trains until both were displaced by the Ivatt Atlantics, which began to appear in 1898 (see **226**). The last 2-2-2 batch had 7ft 7½in driving wheels and 18 × 26in cylinders. These engines were later rebuilt by Ivatt with domed boilers.

30 James Holden built 21 2-2-2s for the Great Eastern between 1889 and 1893. They had short lives, all being scrapped between 1901 and 1907. They had 7ft 0in driving wheels and 18 × 24in cylinders.

29

30

31 There were many other designs of 2-2-2 built during the 1870s and 1880s, amongst which were several varieties on the Great Western. These culminated in the forerunner of the Dean 4-2-2s (see **42**); indeed the first 28 of the later engines were originally built as 2-2-2s, for example *Flying Dutchman* of 1892. All the 2-2-2s were later converted to 4-2-2s.

31

32

33

Particularly outstanding among this class were Nos 3021–3028, which came out in 1891 and ran for a short time on the 7ft 0in broad gauge until its abolition in 1892, the wheels being placed temporarily outside the frames (**32**). They were subsequently converted to standard gauge (similar to *Flying Dutchman*); No 3024 ran in this form until 1894, when it became a 4-2-2 with the name *Storm King* and lasted until 1909.

2-2-2T

33 A historic locomotive which survived into compara-tively recent years was the single-wheel well tank which ran on the Waterford & Tramore Railway in Southern Ireland. It was one of a couple built in 1855 by Fairbairn & Sons. One of them was scrapped by the Great Southern in 1928 but the second, as GSR 483, was still hard at work until 1936, when it was derailed whilst travelling at speed and plunged down an embankment. Unfortunately it was cut up on the spot, otherwise it might well have qualified for preservation. At the time of its demise it was the last single-wheeler in regular passenger service in Great Britain and Ireland; photo-graphed at Tramore in 1932. This 7½ mile line, without intermediate stations, was entirely isolated from the main system. It was closed in 1960. No 483 had 5ft 0in driving wheels, 13 × 19in cylinders and weighed 26 tons (12 tons on driving wheels).

2-2-4T

34 North Eastern Railway *Aerolite*, now to be seen in York Museum, started life in 1869 as a 2-2-2WT de-signed by E. Fletcher. In 1886 it was rebuilt as a side

34

British designs, notably the Midland Johnson Spinners and the GWR Dean singles.

35 The first of Patrick Stirling's '8 footers', No 1, emerged from Doncaster works in 1870. The type was perpetuated in small batches in the following years, so that by the end of 1895 there were 53 of them. The later ones had slightly increased dimensions, the cylinders being enlarged from 18 × 28in to 19½ × 28in. The actual diameter of the driving wheels was 8ft 1in, and they were the only engines designed by Stirling to have outside cylinders or leading bogies. They worked the principal expresses on the GNR, together with the 2-2-2s (see **29**) until the turn of the century, and thereafter gravitated to less arduous work such as cross-country trains on the easily graded routes in Lincolnshire. Some of them were rebuilt by Ivatt with domed boilers, and the last one in service ran until 1916.

The famous No 1, withdrawn in 1907, was stored for several years in Kings Cross shed, but eventually found a

tank, but again transformed in 1892 by William Worsdell to a 4-2-2T as a Worsdell von Borries compound (see **46**). This wheel arrangement was reversed in 1902; the engine became a 2-2-4T as illustrated, in which form it ran until 1933 hauling an official inspectors' saloon. It was subsequently placed in York Museum. It had 5ft 7¾in wheels; the cylinders comprised one high-pressure 13 × 20in and one low-pressure 18½ × 20in, a result of its transformation into a compound.

The NER had three other somewhat similar 2-2-4Ts, not compounds, which remained in service until 1936–7. They were employed mainly on departmental duties, but occasionally on passenger trains. These were the last single-wheelers in service in Great Britain.

4-2-2

The 4-2-2 single-wheeler was not a very widely used type, although its ranks included some of the most famous and to many eyes the most handsome of all

35

place in York Museum, where it may now be seen. It was brought out in 1938 to work several commemorative trips, including one organised by the Railway Correspondence & Travel Society, the first ever privately chartered train for railway enthusiasts.

36 Not unlike the Stirlings in appearance were Bromley's GER engines of which twenty were built between 1879 and 1882, with 7ft 6in driving wheels. They had short lives, all being scrapped by 1893.

For the next few years practically no new single-wheeler designs appeared. The invention of steam sanding gear in 1886 however overcame to a considerable extent their main drawback, lack of sufficient adhesion to start trains of more than 150 tons or so in wet weather. Singles were given a new lease of life, and several designs of 4-2-2 were produced during the ensuing years.

37

36

37 Outstandingly among these new singles were Johnson's Midland Spinners, as they came to be known. Loveliest of engines, 95 were built in five varieties with slight dimensional differences between 1887 and 1900. Successive batches had driving wheels 7ft 4½in, 7ft 6½in, and 7ft 9¼in, cylinders ranging from 18 × 26in to 19½ × 26in, and boiler pressure stepping up from 160lb to 180lb in the last ten. These latter comprised the

38

Princess of Wales class, the initial engine being one of only two Midland engines ever to bear a name. Originally No 2601, later 685, it is illustrated in its original condition. The very large tenders, necessary before the construction of pick-up troughs, were nicknamed 'water carts'. Rather oddly, the later engines were amongst the first casualties, being withdrawn between 1919 and 1921, whilst many of the earlier ones lasted well into the later 1920s.

Last survivor of all was No 673 of 1899, withdrawn in 1928, and set aside for preservation. It had a narrow squeak in 1932, but fortunately survived, and after several years' storage at various locations, was restored to its early condition as No 118. It has now resumed its 1907 identity; in working order, it is on loan from the national collection to the Midland Railway Trust at Swanwick, near Ripley (**38**).

The Spinners were however not quite the first of the new breed of singles. In 1877 three broad gauge Bristol & Exeter 4-2-4Ts (see **47**) were rebuilt as inside-framed 4-2-2 tender engines, the boiler and fittings being almost identical with those of Gooch's Iron Duke class.

39 The Great Northern of Ireland obtained two 4-2-2 engines from Beyer Peacock in 1885 for the Belfast–Dublin mail trains, Nos 88 *Victoria* and 89 *Albert*. They were entirely reconstructed as 4-4-0s in 1904. They were incidentally the only 4-2-2s ever to run in Ireland.

39

40 Scotland's only 4-2-2 was a 'one off' engine built by Neilson & Co. in 1886 for the Edinburgh exhibition, after which it was acquired by the Caledonian Railway. Dugald Drummond, then chief mechanical engineer, obviously had a hand in the design, as it embodied several of his characteristic features. The engine put in many years of useful service on main line trains. It

participated in the 1888 'Race to Scotland' between the east and west coast routes, on which it achieved a daily average of 107¾ minutes over the 100¾ miles between Carlisle and Glasgow, including the nine-mile ascent of Beattock bank with gradients between 1 in 74 and 1 in 88. This was with a light load of four coaches.

After the First World War it was put to work hauling the directors' saloon but in 1930 reverted to ordinary service working light trains on the easy line between Perth and Dundee. This was the last working of an express single-wheeler in ordinary traffic in the British Isles, probably in the world. On withdrawal in 1935 it was restored to CR blue livery and preserved in St Rollox works until 1958, when it was given a complete overhaul and put to work on enthusiasts' specials. On this job it ranged far and wide, not only in Scotland, but south of the border as far afield as the Bluebell Railway in Sussex. In 1966 it was placed in Glasgow Transport Museum, where it can now be seen.

Originally CR No 123, later 1123, it became LMS 14010 at the grouping, eventually to be restored to its Caledonian state, but not quite original condition, as it was built with a Drummond type boiler with safety valves on the dome. The driving wheels were 7ft in diameter, the cylinders 18 × 26in, and the boiler pressure 150lb.

41 The North Eastern was another railway which reverted to the construction of single-wheelers after a lapse of 25 years. These took the form of two classes of 4-2-2 two-cylinder Worsdell von Borries compounds built by T. W. Worsdell, ten with 7ft 1¼in driving wheels built between 1888 and 1890, and another ten with 7ft 7¼ drivers built in 1889 and 1890. The first lot had one high pressure 18 × 24in cylinder and one low pressure 26 × 24in, the corresponding dimensions in the second series being 20 × 24in and 28 × 24in respectively.

After about ten years they were all rebuilt as simple engines with two cylinders, respectively 18in and 19in diameter and with 24in stroke in the two classes. They were broken up between 1918 and 1920.

The second series seem to have been very fine engines in their compound state. No 1518 is stated to have been the first engine in Great Britain to attain a speed of as much as 86 mph, this on the level and not downhill, with a train of 18 six-wheel coaches.

42 Dean's very fine singles for the GWR were extremely handsome engines like their Midland contemporaries. There were ultimately 80 of them, Nos 3001–3080, but 3031 *Achilles* was the first to be built as a 4-2-2, in 1894. Nos 3001–3030 were rebuilds of 2-2-2s constructed between 1891 and 1892, some of which ran for a short time on the broad gauge (**31**, **32**). The last of the class appeared in 1899.

These engines worked for several years on main line expresses, chiefly between Paddington and Newton Abbot, but by the turn of the century they were being gradually allocated to lighter duties and being replaced by coupled engines. All had gone by the end of 1915. A few were rebuilt with Swindon domeless boilers, to the detriment of their handsome outlines. They had 7ft 8½in driving wheels and 19 × 24in cylinders.

43 Holden built ten 4-2-2s for the Great Eastern Railway in 1898. They had 7ft 0in driving wheels, but their low adhesion weight proved insufficient for the increasing formation of the trains, and they never achieved any great prominence. All were scrapped between 1907 and 1910.

44 On the Great Northern, Ivatt introduced a new design of 4-2-2 very different from that of his predecessor Stirling, with 7ft 8in driving wheels and 19 × 26in inside cylinders. 12 engines in all were built between 1898 and 1901, of which the final one, No 270, was the last ever

45

43

44

single-wheeler express engine to be built for use in this country. All were somewhat prematurely withdrawn by Gresley at one fell swoop in 1917.

45 Although not quite the last of the type to be built, these being the GNR engines mentioned above, six engines built to Pollitt's design in 1900 for the Great Central's opened extension to London constituted the last new design ever to be built for use in Britain. (It may be mentioned in passing that as late as 1910 some 4-2-2s were built by Kerr Stuart & Co. of Stoke-on-Trent for the Shanghai–Nanking Railway in China). In 1904 the GCR singles left the London area for the Cheshire Lines Railway to work the express service between Liverpool and Manchester. To this they were very well suited, and they remained on this route until their demise between 1923 and 1927. Nos 5968, 5969 and 5972 survived long enough to be repainted in LNER green livery.

4-2-2T

46 The only engine to run as a 4-2-2T was one of the rebuilds of the NER loco Aerolite (see **34**). In this form it undoubtedly presented a very handsome appearance. A Worsdell von Borries compound, it had one 13 × 20in high-pressure cylinder and one 18½ × 20in low-pressure cylinder; the driving wheels were of 5ft 7¾in diameter. It was converted to a 2-2-4T in 1902.

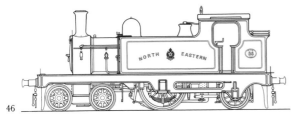

46

4-2-4T

47 The fabulous 4-2-4WTs with 9ft 0in driving wheels built for the broad gauge Bristol & Exeter Railway originated in 1853 with eight engines, numbered 39–46, built by Rothwell & Co. in 1853 to the design of the locomotive superintendent, J. Pearson. The enormous driving wheels, the largest ever used, were situated between two independent swivelling bogies.

Four of them were scrapped in 1868, but the remaining four were completely renewed and fitted with 8ft 10in drivers. Virtually new engines, they were given the numbers 39–42. They became GWR 2001–2004 when that company absorbed the South Devon in 1876, but one was scrapped almost immediately following an accident. The other three were rebuilt as 4-2-2 tender engines in 1877. They lasted in this form until 1884–90.

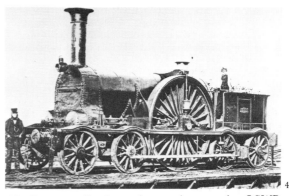

47

48 Drummond's inspection engine on the LSWR (nicknamed *The Bug*) was built in 1899 for his own personal use for touring the system. After his death in 1912 it was little used until 1932, when it was brought out for carrying VIPs around the new docks under construction at Southampton. After this it again went into store at Eastleigh paint shop until it was dismantled in 1940. It had 5ft 7in driving wheels and 11½ × 18in cylinders.

48

0-4-0

49 The 0-4-0 tender engine, dating back to the early years, had become almost entirely obsolete by the turn of the century. Amongst the last to be built were some Wheatley engines on the North British, which appeared in 1869. Three of these were still at work in 1916, and one of them even managed to survive the grouping, being finally scrapped by the LNER in 1925.

Other late survivors were some Glasgow & South Western Stirling engines, of which there were still four in 1916, and one of these lasted until 1922.

50 There are however on the narrow gauge Festiniog Railway three examples of the type. Six engines were built in 1863 and 1867, 0-4-0STs with tenders (originally constructed as 0-4-0Ts). Two of these are unlikely to run again, but it is planned at the time of writing to restore No 2 *Prince* to working order.

50

49

0-4-0T

The tank version of the 0-4-0 arrangement was very widely used, especially by industrial concerns, collieries, steelworks and so on until very recent times, and even today examples may be seen at the few remaining locations where diesel locomotives have not taken over. Most of the main line companies maintained a number for dock shunting and other special duties. The L&YR in 1922 had a total of 61; the Caledonian had 42. There were 38 on the Midland, 36 on the North British, 30 on the LSWR, and 22 on the North Eastern. Most of the other companies however, such as the LNWR, had very few, and they were little used on the GWR, apart from some acquired from the South Wales lines, and there was not a great number of these. On all the Irish railways put together there were but a handful.

51 One very old engine which is still in existence is *Shannon*. It has a very interesting history. Built in 1857 by George English of Hatcham Ironworks for the Sandy & Potton Railway, it later came into the hands of the

LNWR, working for a time on the Cromford & High Peak Railway. In 1878 it was sold to the Wantage Tramway, a roadside line providing connection in the pre-motor age between the Berkshire town of Wantage and Wantage Road on the GWR main line. When the tramway closed in 1945 the engine was restored by the Great Western and placed on a plinth on Wantage Road station. Since then it has been moved to the Didcot Railway Centre of the GWR Society, where it can occasionally be seen in steam.

52 The Lancashire & Yorkshire Railway owned a number of 0-4-0STs which were used for shunting at its various docks. Two of these engines, which were known as Pugs, survive on the Keighley & Worth Valley Railway.

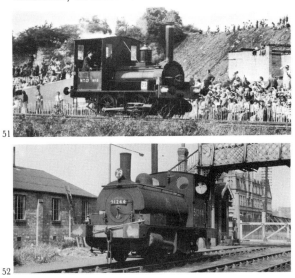

53, 54 On both the Caledonian and the North British their 0-4-0STs were also usually known as Pugs, a popular nickname also met with on other railways, but not necessarily referring to engines of this type. Examples of both CR and NBR engines are illustrated, each with a small wagon attached carrying a running board for the convenience of the shunting men engaged in busy yard operations. One of the NBR type is preserved at Lytham museum.

55 The Midland had 28 0-4-0STs, built between 1883 and 1903, Nos 1500–1527. They were a little unusual in that this type of engine usually had outside cylinders, but then the Midland was always a strictly inside-cylinder line. These 0-4-0STs were also peculiar in being almost the only saddle tanks the MR ever had. Amongst their various duties there were always a number of them to be seen shunting through the streets of Burton-on-Trent to the breweries of that town. The last one disappeared in 1958.

55

56

56 In 1907 there emerged from Derby five side tanks, Nos 1528–1532, again of untypical Midland practice in having outside cylinders, and also Walschaerts valve gear. These two features were to appear on only one other Derby design, the 0-10-0 of 1919. This latter engine, together with the 0-4-0Ts (five more of which came out in 1921, Nos 1533–1537) and the famous compounds, were the only outside-cylinder engines of pure Derby vintage. Two of these 0-4-0Ts survived until as late as 1966. They had 3ft 9¾in wheels, 15 × 22in cylinders, and a boiler pressure of 160lbs.

57 24 side tanks were built by Adams and Drummond for the LSWR between 1891 and 1908. For many years 14 of them were allocated to Southampton Docks, and unusually for the South Western in later years, given names, one of them being No 95 *Honfleur*. Several were sold out of service to industrial concerns, and two have been preserved. No 96 *Normandy* is to be found on the Bluebell Railway, and 102, Formerly *Granville*, is at Bressingham Hall.

59 A Great Eastern 0-4-0ST built in 1903 was latterly used at Stratford Works as works engine. The coal bunker straddled the boiler behind the ogee-shaped saddle tank instead of being in the more usual position to the rear of the cab. It lasted until 1948.

58 On the SE&CR there were a couple of 0-4-0Ts fitted with cranes, a not unusual adaptation of the type. Cranes were more often fitted on 0-6-0Ts however, and usually on industrial railways.

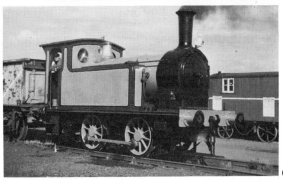

60 A North Eastern 0-4-0T No 1310, built in 1891, is now to be seen on the Middleton Railway, Leeds. It has 3ft 6in wheels, and 14 × 20in cylinders. There were originally 17 of these engines, built between 1887 and 1897. Surprisingly, another five were added to the class in 1923.

61 Six Glasgow & South Western 0-4-0Ts were built between 1907 and 1909 for dock work. No 320 was photographed at Ardrossan in 1925. It became LMS 16048, and was scrapped in 1950.

62

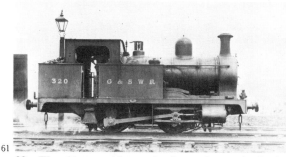

61

62 The oldest working engine in regular service in the British Isles is the 0-4-0WT *Dolgoch* on the 2ft 3in Tal-y-Llyn Railway in Wales. The railway is now operated by a preservation society, inaugurated in 1951 as the first of many such ventures. It was built in 1865 by Fletcher Jennings & Co., and although repaired several times it remains in practically original condition, with its 2ft 3in driving wheels, 8 × 15in cylinders, and 70lb pressure.

63

63 Roadside tramways like the Wantage already mentioned usually had special engines, either 0-4-0Ts or 0-6-0Ts, totally enclosed by a canopy. This gave them the general appearance of a brake van, with side shields covering the wheels to minimise the disturbing effect on horses. LNER 07125, a GER tram engine, was formerly used on the Wisbech and Upwell Tramway which was closed in 1966. The engine had 3ft 1in wheels, 11 × 15in cylinders, and a boiler pressure of 140lbs.

64 The firm of Peckett & Sons of Bristol specialised in engines for industrial use, chiefly 0-6-0STs and 0-4-0STs, and built many hundreds of them for privately-owned firms all over the country. The engine illustrated, typical of the four-wheeled variety, was built in 1907 for the New Westbury Iron Co.

Amongst other firms which concentrated mainly on such engines were Hawthorn Leslie of Newcastle, taken over in 1937 by Robert Stephenson & Co. to form the firm of Robert Stephenson & Hawthorn; Manning Wardle & Co., of Leeds; Andrew Barclay & Co., Kilmarnock; Kerr Stuart & Co., of Stoke-on-Trent; Hudswell Clarke & Co., Leeds; Avonside Engine Co., Bristol; and the Hunslet Engine Co., Leeds, the only one still in business with the facilities for the repair and even building of steam locomotives.

65

64

65 In the 1880s, 1890s, and the earlier part of the present century the Hunslet Engine Co. built a very large number of small 0-4-0STs of approximately 1ft 11in gauge for the Dinorwic and Penrhyn slate quarry systems in North Wales. These were in operation and almost entirely steam worked up to the 1960s. The engines are of particular interest today, as the widespread demand for them during the decline of the steam age has ensured that some 30 of them have survived for preservation. They are now to be seen at various sites around the country, some in working order, whilst several even went to the USA. Full details can be found in the various publications dealing with preserved railways and locomotives. *Alice* is a typical example of the type, and was photographed at the Dinorwic quarries at Llanberis in 1954. General dimensions of the class are 2ft 1in driving wheels, 10½ × 12in cylinders, pressure usually around 140lb and weight around 12½ tons.

66 Also built in considerable numbers for use on industrial lines in the last century were vertical boiler

66

engines, usually known as 'Coffee Pots', of varying patterns. One of the last in use was *Chaloner* of the Pen-y-Orsedd slate quarry, photographed lying derelict there in 1956. It was eventually purchased privately and restored to working order. It may now be seen in steam on the two foot gauge Leighton Buzzard Light Railway.

Chaloner was built by the firm of de Winton in 1877, who constructed some 50 of these little engines between 1869 and 1897. It has 1ft 8in wheels and 6¼ × 12in cylinders. Several others have survived and can be seen in museums and various other locations.

67 Messrs Aveling & Porter, of Rochester, Suffolk, built a good many geared engines embodying a single cylinder with flywheel for industrial firms. They were similar to the road traction engines in which the company later specialised. The earliest known engines of this type came out in 1865; the last one appeared as late as 1924. They were particularly popular in the chalk pits in Kent. A few have been preserved, a good example being *Sydenham*, from the British Oil & Cake Mills, Erith. It is now to be seen at Quainton Road.

67

68

68 A special type of locomotive developed for use on industrial premises with a considerable fire risk was the fireless engine. What is apparently the boiler is in fact a steam reservoir, filled with hot water at very high pressure, usually around 220lb; steam is fed to the cylinders at about 80lb through a reducing valve. The engine can usually work for two or three hours before a necessary visit to the re-charging plant.

Victor was built by Bagnall in 1929 for the Bowater paper mills at Sittingbourne, Kent.

0-4-2

69 The 0-4-2 tender engine came into popularity on a few railways during the latter half of the nineteenth century as a general purpose mixed traffic engine suitable for all kinds of duties. Patrick Stirling may be said to be the innovator of such a standard 'common usage' design of locomotive when he introduced the type to the Glasgow & South Western in 1856. At one time or another this railway possessed no fewer than 164 such engines, the last of which was built in 1878. 55 survived the grouping, most of them having been rebuilt with domed boilers. They were allocated LMS Nos 17021–17075, the last survivor going in 1931.

69

70

71

70 Patrick Stirling went to the Great Northern in 1867, where he perpetuated the type with some very similar engines, 154 in all. The dimensions remained fairly constant throughout their career with 5ft 7½in driving wheels; 17 × 24in cylinders, later enlarged to 17½ × 24in; and 140lb pressure. Ivatt rebuilt ten of them with domed boilers in 1902, but otherwise they remained practically unchanged. A few were still at work in 1920, but none survived the grouping.

71 Apart from the Glasgow & South Western and Great Northern Railways, the largest user of the 0-4-2 tender engine was the London & South Western Railway. Adams brought out his Jubilee class in 1887, Jubilee Year. By 1895 there were 90 of them, Nos

527–556 and 597–656. Drummond eventually replaced the distinctive Adams stovepipe chimneys with his own lipped style, and a number received his boiler with pop safety valves on the dome; otherwise they underwent little change in appearance.

They were to be seen all over the system on every kind of work, and with their 6ft 1in driving wheels they had a considerable turn of speed. Right through to the 1920s there was a regular link of them working from Guildford and Reading on the commuter trains to Waterloo, and No 622 worked the *Atlantic Coast Express* on one occasion in an emergency. Withdrawal commenced in 1928, but was gradual over the ensuing years, and four of them managed to survive into nationalisation. All of these went during 1948.

72 Stroudley on the LB&SCR was the only engineer to use the 0-4-2 for main line express work. Doubts were expressed in some quarters about the use of large 6ft 6in coupled wheels at the front end, with no bogie or even leading pony truck, for high speed; these doubts proved to be unfounded and there is no record of any derailment. The idea however was never followed on any other railway. The cylinders were 19¾ × 26in and the working pressure 140lb, later increased to 150lb. 36 of the Gladstones, as they were known, after the name of the first engine, were built between 1882 and 1891, and they performed fine work on the Brighton main line for many years.

Ten of the engines were withdrawn just prior to the First World War. No further scrappings took place until 1923, when the remaining 26 were gradually taken out of service, the last in 1933. *Gladstone* itself, on withdrawal in 1927, was restored to original condition through the

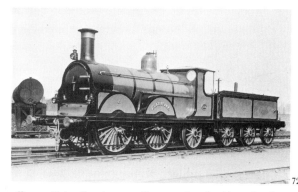

72

efforts of the Stephenson Locomotive Society, the first ever privately sponsored scheme of locomotive preservation. It found a home in York Museum, and is now part of the NRM collection at its new premises in that city.

The Gladstones themselves had been preceded by some very similar engines, and also a mixed traffic version with 5ft 6in driving wheels.

73 0-4-2 engines with outside cylinders were rare, but until 1883 engines with inside cylinders were almost non-existent on the Caledonian Railway. The 0-4-2 was introduced to this line by Benjamin Connor in 1865. The later examples were built during the superintendency of George Brittain between 1878 and 1881, and 21 of them remained at the time of the grouping as LMS 17000–17020. No 17018, photographed at Dundee in 1930, was one of the last survivors. The engines had 5ft 2in driving wheels and 17 × 24in cylinders.

74 The passenger engines of the small Maryport & Carlisle Railway consisted of a few 2-4-0s and 0-4-2s. No 16, built in 1895, was scrapped in 1928. It was one of four which survived into the LMS days as Nos 10010–10013. These engines had 5ft 7½in driving wheels, and 17 × 24in cylinders.

75 The last 0-4-2 tender engine to be built in the British Isles was for the Waterford & Central Ireland Railway. No 4, which became Great Southern & Western Railway 252 on absorption in 1900, was built in 1897 and scrapped in 1909.

73

75

0-4-2T

76 The 0-4-2T was adopted on a number of railways, more particularly in the south. Both the London Chatham & Dover and the South Eastern introduced the type in the 1860s for their London suburban services. The LC&DR engines were well tanks, designed by William Martley. 14 were built by Neilson & Co. in 1866, some very similar engines being supplied by the same makers to the GNR to the design of A. Sturrock. Known as the Scotchmen, the LC&DR engines all bore names of Scottish origin. These were Nos 81–94, to become SE&CR 540–553 in 1899, and they were in service until between 1904 and 1909.

Six more of the same type were built, but with inside frames in place of the outside frames of the earlier series. They were known as the Large Scotchmen (**77**), although inappropriately in this case, as their names had

74

76

77 *524*

no Scottish connection, apart from being built in Scotland by the same makers in 1873. These were Nos 95–100, later SE&CR 554–559, and the last of them ran until 1914. All eventually lost their names, but a few

managed to retain them into SE&CR days, these being the only engines to bear names in the lifetime of that company.

The illustrations show the former 88, *Clyde*, photographed in about 1906, after becoming SE&CR 547; and Large Scotchman No 95 *Albion*.

78 Apart from the Gladstones, Stroudley's finest engines for the LB&SCR, not forgetting his famous Terriers, were probably the D class 0-4-2Ts. The first came out in 1873, and the class had reached a total of 125 by 1887. These remarkable locomotives bore the brunt of the busy suburban traffic until the introduction of eight-wheeled locomotives, 0-4-4Ts and 0-6-2Ts, by his successor R. Billinton in 1892 and 1894. Even so, many of the D tanks continued to take their share until after the First World War, when most of them were drafted to country areas and after the grouping to other parts of the Southern system. They changed considerably in detail

78

79

80

in later years (**79**). One engine received a much larger boiler (**80**). Most of the later survivors were fitted with push-pull apparatus for motor working. Although a few withdrawals took place as early as 1903, 112 of them still remained at the grouping, and a few at nationalisation, the last one going in 1951. It is a great pity that one did not survive for preservation, considering the number of Stroudley's more famous Terriers which have been saved. Their original dimensions were driving wheels: 5ft 6in; cylinders: 17 × 24in; and pressure: 140lb, later increased to 160lb.

81

after 1905 when they lost their names, and the distinctive yellow livery, shown in the illustration of No 239 *Patcham* as first built, was replaced by Marsh's umber. Variations in the boiler mountings, particularly the dome, owing to reboilering, together with the gradual disappearance of the copper-capped chimney resulted in a fascinating variety, as illustrated by the photograph of SR No 2226

81 The Great Western was a very large user of the 0-4-2T. The type was first introduced by Armstrong in 1868, and construction continued steadily until 1897, by which time there were 166 of them. 154 were still in service at the grouping. In 1932, when Collett was locomotive superintendent, the Great Western's policy of replacing old but useful engines with new ones of virtually the same design with a few minor improvements resulted in the appearance of another 95; Nos

82

83

system until the 1950s, when they began to succumb to the inevitable diesel railcar, not to mention branch line closures. The last withdrawal took place in 1964, but four have survived, Nos 1420 and 1450 at work on the Dart Valley, 1466 at Didcot Steam Centre and 1442 on static exhibition at Tiverton. The engines had 5ft 2in driving wheels, 16 × 24in cylinders, and a pressure of 165lb.

83 Eight 0-4-2ST crane engines were built between 1892 and 1895 for the LNWR, two of which survived until 1947. They had 4ft 0in driving wheels. No 3247 was photographed at Crewe works in 1931.

84 The North London had a solitary crane engine of ancient origin, built in 1858 as a 0-4-0ST for the North & South West Junction Railway. Converted to an 0-4-2ST crane engine at Bow in 1872, it had 3ft 10in driving wheels and 13 × 17in cylinders. The oldest engine to be inherited by British Railways in 1948, it was scrapped in 1951 as BR 58865.

4800–4874 (later 1400–1474) fitted with push-pull apparatus (**82**), and Nos 5800–5819.

These engines continued to be seen all over the GWR

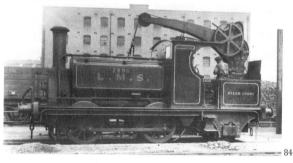

84

85

85 Four 0-4-2Ts of two sizes were built in 1915 by the GNoSR for shunting on the quayside at Aberdeen Harbour. All were scrapped between 1956 and 1960. Nos 68190–1 had 3ft 6in driving wheels and 13 × 20in cylinders. They weighed 25 tons 17 cwt. Nos 68192–3 had 4ft 0in driving wheels and 14 × 20in cylinders. They weighed 30 tons 18 cwt.

86 The Snowdon Mountain is Britain's only rack railway. It is still steam operated by seven of the original eight 0-4-2Ts, of two classes. No 2 *Enid* is one of the earlier variety. Gauge: 2ft 7½in; driving wheels:

2ft 1¾in; rack pinions: 1ft 10¼in diameter; cylinders: 11¾ × 23¾in; pressure 200lb.

0-4-4T

For local passenger working in the later years of the nineteenth century and the earlier decades of the twentieth, the most popular types were eight-wheeled engines, either 0-4-4T or 2-4-2T, the 0-6-2T being a third favourite.

So far as the four-coupled designs were concerned, preference was fairly evenly divided. The Midland, LSWR, SE&CR and Caledonian were exclusively in favour of the 0-4-4T; the L&YR and LNWR built only 2-4-2Ts and the GER, which had tried 0-4-4Ts, also decided on 2-4-2Ts. The North Eastern employed both, but eventually came down more on the side of the 0-4-4T.

87

86

87 At the time of the grouping the Midland had 226 0-4-4Ts, the largest total of any railway, but closely followed by the LSWR and SE&CR, almost equal with 215 and 213 respectively.

The earliest MR engines were the work of Matthew Kirtley. They were double-framed well tanks, of which 26 were built by Messrs Beyer Peacock and Dübs & Co. in 1869–1870. They were long-lived engines and most of them spent all their careers in the London area; their last years were spent mainly working empty stock trains. There they could be seen as late as 1934, by which time they had a somewhat archaic appearance in a great terminus of the metropolis such as St Pancras. They had somehow become part of the scene, and after their demise the grand old station never seemed quite the same without them. No 1205 was photographed at St Pancras in 1920.

88 Johnson followed up the type with his own side tank version with inside frames, of which 205 examples were built between 1875 and 1900 (he had introduced the type on the GER in 1872). They were to be seen all over the system, those allocated to the London area having condensing pipes fitted over the side tanks for working through the Metropolitan tunnels, as in the photograph of No 1315 at Kentish Town. This particular engine also had a Belpaire firebox with pop safety valves in place of the Salter valves on the dome, as originally found on all of Johnson's engines up to 1900. The last survivor went in 1960. The driving wheels were 5ft 4in in diameter (5ft 7in on the earlier ones). The cylinders were 18 × 24in.

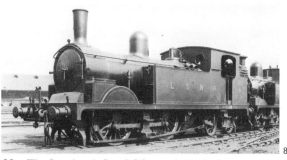

89

89 The London & South Western's total of 215 0-4-4Ts was made up of two classes designed by William Adams and one by Dugald Drummond. Adams abandoned the 4-4-2T type for suburban work in favour of the 0-4-4T in 1888; he built 50 examples with 5ft 7in driving wheels between that year and 1896, known generally as the T1 class. They were withdrawn between 1931 and 1951.

90 Adams followed the T1 with a smaller 4ft 10in version, the O2, designed mainly for branch line work

88

44

90

and general shunting duties. Right up to the early 1930s some of them could always be seen marshalling carriage stock in Clapham Junction sidings.

In 1923 two of them were sent over to the Isle of Wight for trials, and proved so successful that eventually 23 of them were so transferred, the last as late as 1949. The class eventually took over all the working on the island, on which they remained until the virtual closing of all the railways there in 1966. They were renumbered W14–W36 and all acquired names of local interest. One such engine, No W19 *Osborne*, is shown in the photograph at Ryde in 1931. They later received extended bunkers to increase coal capacity, but otherwise the only alteration of any significance to the class as a whole, including those running on the mainland, was the provision of Drummond boilers with dome-top safety valves. Not all were so modified however, and in the Isle of Wight most of them reverted to the Adams type, which were found more satisfactory.

Withdrawal commenced in 1933, but many of the class lasted until the 1950s and several of those in the Isle of

91

91 Dugald Drummond continued the construction of 5ft 7in engines in 1896 with his own modified version, the M7. The chief difference was the use of his own boiler with dome safety valves and lip style chimney, together with an increase in the cylinder dimensions from 18in to 18½ × 26in, and in boiler pressure from 160lb to 175lb. There were 105 of these engines in all, the last coming out in 1911; all were virtually identical. They remained practically unchanged throughout their existence except for one engine, No 126, which Urie rebuilt with a superheater and extended smokebox. This resulted in a somewhat ungainly locomotive with a reputation for instability, and no more were so treated. It was scrapped in 1937, many years before any of the unrebuilt engines (the next withdrawal occurred in 1948, the result of an accident).

Initially the M7s were tried out on the main line between Exeter and Plymouth, but after a derailment at speed they were taken off express working. Until the commencement of electrification in 1915 most of them were in the London area, but subsequently many migrated to country districts, a lot of them being fitted with push-pull apparatus for branch line working. A good many of them lasted until the 1960s and No 245 has been preserved and can be seen in the National Railway Museum at York.

92 At the 1899 amalgamation the South Eastern & Chatham acquired a large number of 0-4-4Ts from both of its constituents, the South Eastern and the London Chatham & Dover. The LC&DR provided 54 of four slightly different versions, and another 15 came out in 1900 as SE&CR engines, but virtually of Kirtley's design. All but one of the original LC&DR engines lasted into the grouping era, but disappeared in the 1920s. Out of the final 15 a few even survived nationalisation, the last one going in 1956.

One of these, No A703 was photographed at Slades

Green in 1925. It had 5ft 6in driving wheels with 17½ × 24in cylinders. The dimensions of the earlier ones were much the same except that some of them had smaller driving wheels of 5ft 3in.

93

93 The SER engines, 118 in all designed by James Stirling, had the inevitable domeless boilers, a feature of all locomotives designed by the Stirling brothers. They had 5ft 6in driving wheels, and 18 × 26in cylinders. Quite a number of these engines were scrapped from 1907 onwards, but the majority survived to become Southern engines in 1923, the last remaining in service until 1930. Most of them had by this time been rebuilt by Wainwright with domed boilers. No 410, still in SE&CR wartime grey livery, was photographed in 1924.

94 Mr H. S. Wainwright, who had been appointed locomotive superintendent of the newly-formed South Eastern & Chatham Railway in 1899, produced his own

92

94

0-4-4T for suburban services in 1903, carrying on the traditions of his predecessors on the two constituent railways. The first of these appeared in 1904, and the last in 1915, by which time they totalled 66. The general dimensions were not greatly different from their ancestors, having 5ft 6in driving wheels, and 18 × 26in cylinders, but the new engines were slightly larger and heavier, with increased working pressure.

They remained practically unaltered apart from changes of painting style and livery at the grouping, and again at nationalisation, which nearly all of them survived. No 5 (as SR A5) was photographed at Gillingham in 1930. No 263 has been preserved in its original livery and can be seen at work on the Bluebell Railway.

95 In 1895 McIntosh produced an 0-4-4T for sub-

urban and branch line work on the Caledonian Railway. By 1915 there were 110 of them, all of the same basic design but successively enlarged. They had 5ft 6in driving wheels and 19 × 26in cylinders. The design proved so successful that not only did Pickersgill, McIntosh's successor, add a further ten in 1922, but yet another ten appeared in 1925 after the grouping, coming out new as LMS 15260–15269. Most of the later ones lasted well into BR days. No 15189 has been restored to CR blue livery as No 419 by the Scottish Railway Preservation Society, and can be seen at their premises at Falkirk.

McIntosh also built a smaller version in 1899 with 4ft 6in driving wheels, known as the Balerno tanks. His engines were not the first 0-4-4Ts on the CR, as there had been some ancient outside-cylinder engines built by Connor in 1873, and Drummond had introduced the inside-cylinder type in 1884 with a series of 15 engines designed for branch line work.

95

96 Wilson Worsdell's 1894 design of 0-4-4T for the North Eastern Railway followed Fletcher's well tanks, which had been introduced in 1874. There were ultimately 110 of them built up to the year 1901. They became LNER class G5, passing into BR ownership as

47

96

97

had been two Fairlie 0-4-4Ts on the Great Southern & Western in Ireland in 1869, but with inside cylinders.) It was also of historical importance in being almost the first application of Walschaert's valve gear in this country. It had 5ft 6in driving wheels and 16 × 22in cylinders, but appears to have done little work. It spent most of its life in a siding, where the only known photograph appears to have been taken, and quietly faded away into oblivion.

98 A series of somewhat unusual-looking 0-4-4WTs were built by Aspinall on the GS&WR in Ireland between 1871 and 1884, most of which survived into the 1930s and one until 1945. They had 5ft 7½in wheels and 15 × 22in cylinders. Two earlier engines of almost identical appearance had been built on the Fairlie principle, with a swivelling steam bogie.

98

67240–67349. All of them had disappeared by the end of the 1950s, largely owing to the advent of the diesel railcar. They had 5ft 1¼in driving wheels, and 18 × 24in cylinders.

97 A unique locomotive, built in 1878, was acquired in 1881 for the Swindon, Marlborough & Andover Junction Railway (later the Midland and South Western Junction). In the first place, it was a Fairlie engine, in which the coupled wheels and cylinders formed a separate swivelling bogie, independent of the main frames. (There

99 The last 0-4-4Ts to be built were a series of ten engines designed for the LMS. They came out as late as 1932, shortly after the appointment of William Stanier as Chief Mechanical Engineer. They were in effect a slightly enlarged version of the Midland Railway Johnsons, many of which were 50 years or more old, and in need of replacement. This was much in the Great Western

99

Railway tradition (Stanier had just come from Swindon) as exemplified by the 0-4-2Ts built for that railway in 1932 (see **81**). All Stanier's 0-4-4Ts were scrapped by 1962.

2-4-0

The 2-4-0 was the standard express type on almost every main line for very many years during the second half of the nineteenth century, until gradually displaced by larger engines, at first by 4-4-0s, which in turn gave way to 4-4-2, 4-6-0, and eventually 4-6-2 types. As all the principal railways in the British Isles used 2-4-0s of many varieties, it is only possible to illustrate a selection of the most interesting and more important of them.

100 Amongst the earliest examples, which began to appear in the 1850s, the most outstanding were probably those of Joseph Beattie, built in considerable numbers for the London & South Western. The earlier ones were designed for goods work, with 5ft 0in or 5ft 6in driving wheels, but from 1859 onwards Beattie produced several classes for passenger duties. All of his 2-4-0s had outside

100

101

cylinders, unusual at that time and indeed for many years afterwards, and while most had driving wheels of 6ft 0in or 6ft 6in, a few of them had 7ft 0in, then the largest coupled wheels to appear in this country. One of the latter, No 97 *Pegasus*, was photographed soon after its construction in 1868. It lasted until 1898.

101 22 2-4-0s, of an early design by Kirtley, were built for the Midland Railway between 1866 and 1873. They were long-lived engines, and the last one to remain in service in 1947, LMS No 20002 as it had by then become, was fortunately secured for preservation through the efforts of the Stephenson Locomotive Society. Now restored to its earlier condition as MR 158A, it can be seen at the premises of the Midland Railway Trust at Swanwick, near Ripley, Derbyshire.

102 Kirtley designed a class of 2-4-0s with 6ft 8in driving wheels for express working on the Midland Railway. The first of these engines appeared in 1870; the last was scrapped in 1936.

102

103 S. W. Johnson, who succeeded Kirtley in 1873, preferred inside frames to the outside frames favoured by his predecessor, and all of his handsome designs followed this pattern. He continued the construction of 2-4-0s until 1881, after which he went over to similar engines with leading bogies, 4-4-0s, and also to 4-2-2 single-wheelers for express passenger working.

The 2-4-0s were built in four varieties of different wheel dimensions, 6ft 3in, 6ft 6in, 6ft 9in and 7ft 0in.

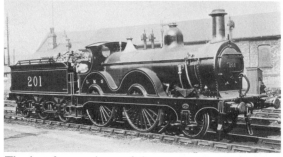

103

The last few survivors of these numerous engines just managed to last into BR days, finally disappearing in 1949. Many of them in later years received Belpaire fireboxes.

104 Patrick Stirling made good use of the 2-4-0 on the Great Northern Railway during his reign of office from 1866 to 1895. He built a number concurrently with his 2-2-2s and famous 4-2-2 eight-footers. He also rebuilt a number of older 2-4-0s designed by his predecessor Archibald Sturrock. His successor Ivatt turned out a final ten in 1897, basically of Stirling's design.

No 890, built in 1893, is typical of Stirling's later engines. A few GNR 2-4-0s survived into the grouping, the last one going in 1927.

105 The Highland was one of the few railways which favoured outside cylinders until the turn of the century. This was the policy of locomotive superintendents William Barclay and David Jones, who were in office between 1855 and 1896 (with William Stroudley in

104

105

106 John Ramsbottom's 2-4-0 express engine for the LNWR first appeared in 1866, and an old view of No 1211, named after its designer, shows the engine in original condition. The curved running plate and air vents on the splashers were later modified by Mr F. W. Webb, when he introduced his own design of 2-4-0 in 1873. Thus rebuilt, *John Ramsbottom* survived until 1930 as LMS 5012.

Ten of these engines, built at Crewe in 1873, were supplied to the Lancashire & Yorkshire Railway. One of them, which had been used on departmental duties conveying high-ranking officials around the system in an inspection coach, passed into LMS hands at the grouping as No 10000. It was scrapped in 1926.

106

107 Webb's Precedent class 2-4-0s, which were built in considerable numbers between 1873 and 1896, were renowned for the hard work they put in on the LNWR main line, until the arrival of Whale's Precursors in 1904.

No 790 *Hardwicke*, which distinguished itself in the famous 1895 race to Scotland between the west and east coast routes, was set aside for preservation on its

charge for a short intervening period from 1866–69).

The earlier Barclay 2-4-0s with 5ft 3in driving wheels for goods working featured a distinctive style of framing, allied to the outside cylinders combined with the smokebox. This was derived from Crewe and was originated by Alexander Allan; the style also appeared on the LNWR of the period. No 27, built in 1863, was one of two survivors which managed to survive the grouping, although it was never taken into LMS stock.

107

108

clads, 20 engines built in 1876 at the time of Cudworth's resignation. John Ramsbottom of the LNWR is believed to have been consulted on their design.

No 272 was photographed after the SER and the LC&DR had been amalgamated in 1899 as the SE&CR, and had acquired a Stirling domeless boiler. All were scrapped between 1904 and 1906.

109

withdrawal in 1932, and can be seen in York museum. In recent years it has occasionally been steamed and used on enthusiasts' specials.

108 The South Eastern Railway was a considerable user of 2-4-0s. The most numerous of these was the 118 class designed by James Cudworth, who was locomotive superintendent from 1853 until succeeded by James Stirling in 1883.

No 247 was one of the later examples, having been built in 1874. It was the last survivor of the class when scrapped in 1905. It had been rebuilt in 1896 by Stirling with one of his standard domeless boilers.

109 The South Eastern Railway also had the Iron-

110

110 The London Chatham & Dover employed 2-4-0s for most of its express passenger trains through the superintendency of William Martley, who was in office from 1860 to 1874. His successor William Kirtley continued the type for a few years, but in 1877 he introduced his 4-4-0s, and these gradually took over the main line duties until the amalgamation with the South Eastern as the South Eastern & Chatham Railway in 1899.

No 43 *Hyacinth* was one of Martley's Dawn class, twelve engines built in 1862 and 1863. All survived to become SE&CR engines, *Hyacinth* until 1904, whilst one of them, *Snowdrop*, lasted to 1908; they had lost their names in the meantime.

111 Benjamin Connor produced several designs of 2-4-0 for the Caledonian, between 1865 and 1878. Connor was another of the few designers of this period who favoured outside cylinders for his locomotives, even his 0-6-0 tender engines, such being extremely rare in Britain.

No 1097 (originally 97) was one of a batch of 11 with 6ft 8in wheels built between 1865 and 1867 for semi-fast trains between Glasgow and Carlisle. They were very soon transferred to the former Scottish North Eastern section for main line work, and the last of the class was broken up in 1909.

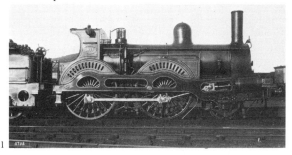

111

112 E. Fletcher was responsible for the construction of several classes of 2-4-0 on the North Eastern, but the best of these were undoubtedly the 901 class of 1872, with 7ft 1¼in driving wheels. These were the principal express engines on the main line for a number of years.

Ten of them survived until LNER days, and No 910, photographed in rebuilt form, was restored on withdrawal in 1925 to its original condition. It can now be seen in York Museum.

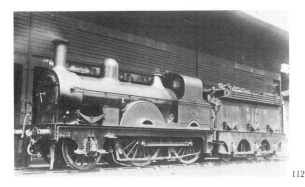

112

113 A later NER design of 2-4-0 was produced in 1885 by a committee under the chairmanship of the general manager, Henry Tennant. One of the class, No 1463, has been preserved and is now in the small museum at North Road Station, Darlington.

114 The Lancashire & Yorkshire was not a great employer of 2-4-0s. None were built after 1876, the year

113

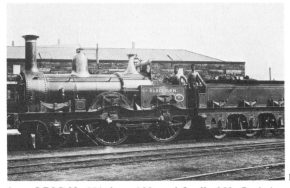

115

114

in which No 92 appeared, one of a batch of 34 constructed over a period of six years. It worked only until 1894, and all of the class had gone by 1899. They were replaced in the 1880s by 4-4-0s.

115 The West Lancashire Railway 2-4-0 No 7 *Blackburn* was originally a LB&SCR engine designed by Craven and built at Brighton in 1862. It had initially

been LBSC No 151, later 120, and finally 363. On being sold to the WLR in 1883 it was given a Stroudley-type number plate before being delivered to its new owners, and it retained its LBSC yellow livery. It was one of a pair to be so delivered, the other being LBSC No 150, which became WLR No 8 *Preston*. The latter was scrapped in 1887 and *Blackburn* in 1890. The WLR eventually became part of the Lancashire & Yorkshire system.

116 The Great Western had many 2-4-0s over the years for both broad and narrow gauge, some of the former having been inherited from the Bristol & Exeter Railway. There were a large number of variations of the type. No 2220 was one of a batch of 20 built in 1881–2. It was photographed at Southall in 1920 in its final form after receiving a Belpaire firebox. It was scrapped in 1921, by which time most of them had already gone, although one lasted until 1926.

116

117

117 In 1885 the GWR built 20 2-4-0Ts with double frames and wheels of only 5ft 1in diameter. They were converted to tender engines, and subsequently underwent various modifications, but No 3514 was the only one to acquire a domeless boiler. It was scrapped in 1929.

118 Three later-surviving 2-4-0s on the GWR had been built by Dübs & Co. in 1894 for the Midland & South Western Junction Railway, Nos 10–12. They were taken over by the Great Western at the grouping. They became Nos 1334–1336, of which the first two were withdrawn in 1952, and No 1336 in 1954. They were thus among the few of the type to become British Railways engines. No 1335 was photographed at Oxford in 1952.

118

119 For many years the Belfast & Northern Counties Railway of Ireland (later to be taken over by the Midland Railway of England and eventually to pass into LMS ownership), under the superintendency of Bowman Malcolm, favoured two-cylinder compounds of the Worsdell von Borries system. This employed two cylinders only, one small high pressure and a second, considerably larger in diameter, to receive the exhaust steam at a lower pressure. A peculiarity of these engines when

119

observed in action was the slow beat of the exhaust, only two to each revolution of the driving wheels in place of the normal four (or six in the case of most three-cylinder engines).

The NCC, as it later became (Northern Counties Committee of the Midland) had a number of these 2-4-0s, some of which were ultimately converted to 4-4-0s. No 57 *Galgorm Castle*, built in 1895, was photographed at Belfast in 1937. It was scrapped in 1938. This particular locomotive was especially noteworthy in that it was the first engine in the world to be fitted with Ross 'pop' safety valves, later to become almost universal on British Railways.

120 The Great Eastern was the first British railway to experiment with oil firing. No 760 *Petrolea*, one of only three Great Eastern engines ever to bear a name, was one of a class of 100 engines built by James Holden between 1886 and 1897. Many of them were fitted for burning oil in 1893 with practical success, but owing to the rise in the price of the fuel it was not a satisfactory economic venture and reversion was made to coal firing. (For later temporary conversions to oil burning see **178**, **179**, **436**.)

These 7ft 0in engines were the principal Great Eastern express engines for several years after their introduction. Between 1902 and 1904, 21 of them were rebuilt with much larger high-pitched boilers. Another 60 were rebuilt similarly but with a leading bogie as 4-4-0s.

120

121

121 James Holden's other design of 2-4-0 for the Great Eastern was a mixed traffic version with 5ft 8in driving wheels, consisting of a hundred engines built between

1891 and 1902. Several of these lasted until BR days, well into the 1950s. No 490 was in fact the last 2-4-0 to run in Great Britain, as distinct from Ireland, and on withdrawal in 1959 it was restored to its original condition and blue livery and can now be seen in York Museum.

122 The Hull & Barnsley Railway had ten 2-4-0s with 6ft 0in wheels, built by Messrs Beyer Peacock & Co. in 1885 to the designs of William Kirtley, of the London Chatham & Dover Railway. Kirtley acted as consultant engineer to the H & B Railway in its earlier years; the H & B was a comparative latecomer on the railway scene, having been constructed during the 1880s.

In due course the position of locomotive engineer was filled by Matthew Stirling, son of the famous Patrick Stirling of the Great Northern Railway. He was in charge from May 1885 until the absorption of the H & BR by the North Eastern in 1922. He rebuilt several of the Kirtley 2-4-0s in the true Stirling tradition with domeless boilers, increasing the pressure from 140lb to 150lb and fitting the distinctive type of Stirling cab favoured by the Stirling family, as illustrated. All of the Hull & Barnsley 2-4-0s had disappeared in 1922.

123 One of the last 2-4-0s to be built was for the small Stratford on Avon and Midland Junction Railway, turned out by Messrs Beyer Peacock & Co. in 1903. It was the SMJ's only 'express' passenger engine, most of its services being worked by 0-6-0s. SMJ No 13 was absorbed by the LMS at the grouping; it was allocated the number 290, which it never carried, and it was scrapped in 1924.

123

122

124

124 The very last new 2-4-0s were on the North Staffordshire Railway, Nos 15 and 54, built at the company's own works at Stoke in 1906. They were only in service until 1920. No 15 was photographed at Llandudno in 1909.

125 The last 2-4-0s of all to run in the British Isles were in Ireland, on Coras Iompair Eireann. They were the survivors of a numerous class built between 1869 and 1897 for the Midland Great Western railway, some of which had been rebuilt as 4-4-0s. One of the original ones, No 6, sported a curious flared cab; an early form of streamlining?

Some of the later survivors were rebuilt with Belpaire fireboxes and superheaters. No 650 was one such, photographed at Bray in 1955 (**126**). The last one to be withdrawn was No 653 in 1963, and it is a great pity that it was not retained for preservation, as no MGWR engine is now in existence.

126

125

127

127 Although not strictly 2-4-0 engines, in that the driving wheels are uncoupled, this is a convenient point to include F. W. Webb's notorious and ill-fated three-cylinder compounds, 2-(2-2)-0s, the first of which appeared in 1882. The story is well known; Webb persisted in building them for several years for main line work on the West Coast route, but they gave endless trouble. Although they could perform well on occasion, recourse often had to be made to the more reliable Precedents (**107**). There were three cylinders, two outside high pressure ones of 14 × 24in driving the rear driving wheels, and one inside low pressure, into which steam from the high pressure cylinders passed before being exhausted by the chimney. This cylinder was of 30in diameter with 24in stroke. It drove the leading pair of driving wheels and it was a not uncommon sight to see the engine try to start its train with the two pairs of driving wheels revolving in opposite directions! The main object was to reduce coal consumption.

The last batch, the Teutonics (illustrated), appeared in 1889. They had 7ft 0in driving wheels, and were probably the best of them. No 1304 *Jeannie Deans* worked the 2.00 pm corridor from Euston to Crewe and the corresponding up 7.32 pm almost continuously from 1891 to 1899, and No 1309 *Adriatic* took part in the 1895 race to Scotland (with a load of only four coaches, about 95 tons). Nevertheless all were ruthlessly consigned to the scrap heap when George Whale succeeded Webb in 1903.

2-4-0T

128   The 2-4-0T was used by a number of railways – for the most part in fairly small numbers – for local passenger work. Of outstanding interest are those of the LSWR, built by Joseph Beattie and his son W. G. Beattie, who succeeded him in 1871. Some earlier ones had appeared between 1856 and 1859, but the principal class consisted of 88 well tanks, built between 1863 and 1875, nearly all by Beyer Peacock & Co. They worked chiefly on the London suburban services until the 1880s, when they were displaced by Adams 4-4-2Ts (see **239**). Most of them were rebuilt as 2-4-0 tender engines.

Both the rebuilds and those remaining as tanks had all

128

disappeared by 1898 with three exceptions, which were retained for working the Wenford Bridge mineral line in Cornwall. These were destined to remain in traffic until 1962, three times as long as any of their sisters. They were rebuilt several times whilst remaining basically the same, the chief differences being the provision of Drummond boilers and chimneys, and steel buffer beams in place of the original wooden ones. On withdrawal in 1962 two of them were saved for preservation, one by British Railways and now on loan to the Dart Valley Railway; the other at Quainton Road, where it was photographed in 1978 as SR 0314.

The engines were built with 5ft 7in driving wheels, 16½ × 20in cylinders, and a boiler pressure of 160lb.

129   Armstrong and Dean constructed a large number of 2-4-0Ts for the GWR between 1869 and 1899. They were usually known as the Metropolitan tanks, as many of them were fitted with condensing apparatus for working through the tunnels on the Metropolitan line; the majority were however found on country branches. There were three successive classes with increased

129

dimensions and tank capacities, but all had 5ft 0in wheels and 16 × 24in cylinders.

They worked the London suburban area services until gradually replaced by 4-4-2Ts and 2-6-2Ts from about 1905 onwards. Nevertheless some of them could still be seen working locals into Paddington in the early 1920s, with a surprising turn of speed in view of their small driving wheels. The last of them disappeared in 1949.

130 On the LNWR Webb built 50 2-4-0Ts between 1876 and 1880. They had 4ft 8½in driving wheels, 17 × 20in cylinders and 150lb pressure. Ten survived the grouping to be allocated LMS Nos 6420–6429; No 6422 was photographed in 1934, two years before being scrapped. No 6428 outlasted all the others by many years on the Cromford & High Peak Railway, being scrapped in 1952 as BR 58092.

131 2-4-0Ts were very rare on the railways which formed the LNER at the grouping; in fact the only ones surviving in 1923 were two of a class of eight outside-framed engines built by Sacré in 1881 for the MS&LR. They were finally employed on the push-pull service between Aylesbury and Verney Junction. They had 5ft 6½in wheels and 16 × 24in cylinders.

No 450B was photographed at Neasden in 1922; the other was No 449B, but both were scrapped without receiving their new LNER Nos 6455 and 6456.

130

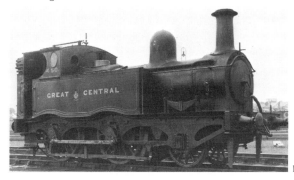

131

132

133

No W13 *Ryde*. On withdrawal in 1932 it was placed aside for preservation, but unfortunately broken up during the war.

133 Four 2-4-0 STs were built in 1883 for the Belfast & Northern Counties Railway, the only broad gauge tank engines on that railway until 1914. No 48 was photographed in 1930, still bearing the initials of the Midland Railway which had taken over the B&NCR in 1903, indicating that it had not received a repaint for 27 years.

134 Mention must be made of the Beyer Peacock 2-4-0Ts built for the 3ft 0in gauge Isle of Man Railway. They were constructed over a long period, the first coming out in 1873 and the last in 1926, by which time there were 15 of them. They had 3ft 6in driving wheels and 12 × 18in cylinders; the later engines were slightly larger, with greater water capacity increasing the weight from 20½ tons to 23 tons 6cwt.

The more recent fortunes, or misfortunes, of the railway have been amply recorded elsewhere; sufficient

132 Throughout its independence, until taken over by the Southern Railway in 1923, the Isle of Wight worked the busy service on its 'main line' between Ryde and Ventnor with seven 2-4-0Ts built between 1864 and 1883. They had 5ft 0in wheels and cylinders varying between 15 × 20in and 17 × 24in. Named after locations on the route, they carried no numbers until the remaining engines were numbered W13 to W18 in the SR list. The last survivor was the original engine

134

to say that at the time of writing four or five of the engines are still in working order operating the summer-only service on the surviving section of the line between Douglas and Port Erin. Most of the remainder are still in existence, but having lain for many years in store they are unlikely to run again.

Two almost identical engines were built in 1877–8 for the Ballymena & Larne Railway in Ireland, one of which survived into the LMS (NCC) era, to be sold later to the Castlederg & Victoria Bridge and scrapped in 1934.

135

2-4-2

135 Although there has never been a standard gauge 2-4-2 tender engine in the British Isles, a very close approximation is to be found in Webb's final design of uncoupled 2-(2-2)-2 compound, an elongated version of his earlier 2-(2-2)-0 (see **127**). Twenty were built for the LNWR in two classes: ten Great Britains with 7ft 1in driving wheels, built in 1891–4; and ten John Hicks with 6ft 3in driving wheels. The latter were intended to work the more hilly section of the line between Crewe and Carlisle, and were built in 1894–8. Although poor engines, they were not scrapped en masse like the 2-(2-2)-0s, and one survived until 1912. The photograph depicts No 525 *Princess May* of the 7ft 1in series.

2-4-2T

By far the largest users of the 2-4-2T were the L&YR, LNWR and GER, and to a lesser extent the NER and the Manchester, Sheffield & Lincolnshire (later GCR).

136 Sir John Aspinall introduced the type to the Lancashire & Yorkshire in 1889, his very successful design being perpetuated by his successors Hoy and Hughes until by 1911 there were no less than 330 of them. The later ones were fitted with Belpaire fireboxes and superheaters, but basically they remained unchanged, having 5ft 8in driving wheels and $17\frac{1}{2} \times 26$in or 18×26in cylinders.

These engines not only monopolised the busy suburban services of the L&Y, but also did a great deal of main-line express work, to which they were eminently suited in view of the comparatively short distances traversed by many of the L&YR's main lines. All passed into the hands of the LMS at the grouping to become Nos 10621 to 10950. Their withdrawal was gradual, and the type lasted well into the 1950s. The original engine No 1008 has been preserved and can be seen in the National Railway Museum, York.

136

137

2-4-2Ts had been reduced to 243. 86 of the small ones were allocated LMS Nos 6515–6600, although not all these survived to be thus renumbered. Nos 6601–6757 were allocated to the larger engines. A few of these survived into BR days; No 46727 was photographed at Craven Arms in 1945. The last one was scrapped in 1955.

They remained virtually unaltered throughout their existence, apart from painting and numbering. They even retained their vintage LNWR chimneys, a feature so often altered in accordance with the style favoured by successive locomotive superintendents.

138 Webb designed an uncoupled compound version of his standard 2-4-2T, a 2-(2-2)-2T under the Whyte classification. Described as a 'patent engine for suburban work', a photograph of No 687, built in 1885, clearly shows the large low-pressure cylinder to the rear of the buffer beam.

In common with other Webb compounds they suffered from an unpleasant fore and aft surging motion when

137 Webb's standard simple 2-4-2Ts for the LNWR were of two classes, 180 engines with 4ft 6in driving wheels and a larger version with 5ft 6in driving wheels, of which 160 came out between 1890 and 1897. 40 of these latter were rebuilds of 2-4-0 tender engines.

By the time of the grouping the LNWR's total of

138

starting. This was particularly noticeable on an engine making frequent stops and starts, and Ahrons recalls a journey on which the unfortunate passengers were swaying backwards and forwards after the manner of a University Eight! Needless to say little more was heard of this effort of Webb's. The same uncomfortable feature was however occasionally experienced many years later when travelling in the front coach behind some Great Western types and even certain standard designs.

139

140

139 After a brief flirtation with the 0-4-4T for suburban work, of which 40 were built by James Holden between 1898 and 1901 (S. W. Johnson had previously used the type on the GER in 1872) he reverted to the 2-4-2T which had already been introduced by Worsdell in 1884–7. The engines he designed were heavy on coal consumption; this characteristic gave rise to the nickname 'Gobblers' which stuck to all of their successors throughout their existence, although not with the same justification.

Later developments of the same basic design were built by J. Holden and his successor S. D. Holden until 1912, culminating in the last ten engines Nos 1–10 (**140**).

All except Nos 1300–1311, built in 1909–10, had driving wheels 5ft 4in or 5ft 8in; the other dimensions were progressively enlarged. These 12, designed for push-pull operation, had 4ft 10in drivers, and because of their very large cabs they were nicknamed 'Crystal Palaces' (**141**).

In all there were 235 2-4-2Ts still in service at the grouping; they continued to work the busy GER sub-

141

urban services alongside the newer N7 0-6-2Ts until eventual electrification. The last survivor went in 1958.

142 Four curious double-ended 2-4-2Ts with dual controls were built in 1906 for the Dublin & Blessington roadside tramway in Ireland by T. Green of Leeds. They were scrapped in 1933 on the closure of the line.

143 The Northern Counties Committee (LMS) in Ireland had several 2-4-2T Von Borries two-cylinder compounds in service on its 3ft gauge lines, the last built as recently as 1920 at the Midland's Derby Works. The design had originated in 1891 on the Ballymena & Larne Railway.

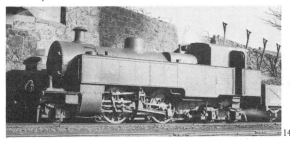

144

142

143

2-4-4T

144 One of the NCC(LMS) 2-4-2Ts was rebuilt in 1931 with a trailing bogie, thus becoming the only 2-4-4T ever to be seen in the British Isles. It was photographed at Larne in 1937. The engine was not a success in this form, and was scrapped in 1946.

4-4-0

The 4-4-0 was to become the most widely used express passenger type during what may be called the middle period of British locomotive development, from the early 1870s until well into the present century. It was gradually to be displaced by larger engines, usually six-coupled, notably the 4-6-0 and ultimately the Pacific, although it was very far from ever suffering total eclipse. Two major railways in particular, the Midland and the South Eastern & Chatham, employed nothing larger for their principal main line trains right up to the grouping in 1923. The Great North of Scotland, after the disappearance of its earlier 2-4-0s in 1909, relied almost entirely on 4-4-0s for its operation, apart from a small stud of 0-4-4Ts for suburban services out of Aberdeen (discontinued in 1937) and a few shunting tanks. Indeed, at the time of the grouping, out of a total stock of 122 engines, no less than 100 were 4-4-0s, and uniquely it never possessed any 0-6-0 tender engines.

Even after the 1923 amalgamation some very fine designs were to appear, notably the Schools class on the Southern, generally regarded as the ultimate achievement in 4-4-0 design. The famous LMS compounds became a standard design for further construction during the early post-grouping period. In Ireland, too, the Great Northern remained faithful to the 4-4-0 for its top link services, and indeed was responsible for the last examples of the type to be built in Britain, as late as 1948.

145 The earliest 4-4-0s to appear were a couple of outside-cylinder engines built by Messrs R. Stephenson

145

& Co. for the Stockton & Darlington Railway in 1860. Nos 160 *Brougham* and 161 *Lowther* had 6ft 0in driving wheels and 16 × 24in cylinders.

They were followed by four 7ft 0in engines built in 1862 to the design of William Bouch, Nos 162 to 165; these were known as the Saltburn class, and were at work until 1879–88.

146

146 Ten fairly similar engines appeared in 1871. Known as Ginx's Babies, S & D Nos 238–241, they were followed by six more in 1874, which came out as NER 1265–1270, this company having by then absorbed the S & D. These were later rebuilt as 2-4-0s, and some of them lasted until 1913–4.

Almost concurrently with the earliest North Eastern engines, the London Chatham & Dover Railway obtained its first new locomotives in the shape of four 4-4-0s built by Hawthorn in 1860–1, followed in 1861–2 by 24 curious machines to the design of T. R. Crampton with the outside cylinders placed amidships driving direct on to the rear coupled wheels. They were found to be more or less useless, and moreover so damaging to the track that they were soon laid aside and virtually scrapped, although parts of them were ultimately used in the construction of some more 2-4-0s.

147

148

The final eight engines came out in 1920–1; for the first time on the GNoSR they were all named. They had 6ft 1in driving wheels with 18×26in cylinders and 160lb pressure. Somewhat small engines for such a comparatively late period, they were quite adequate for the needs of the GNoSR until the grouping, when they were supplanted on the main line by some 4-6-0s from the Great Eastern. They continued to find useful employment however on the lengthy branches of the GNoSR. One of the last to survive was BR 62277. On withdrawal in 1958 it was restored to GNoSR 49 *Gordon Highlander*, and worked for a few years on rail tour specials, after which it was placed in Glasgow museum where it can now be seen (**149**).

149

147 After the North Eastern and London Chatham & Dover, some of the Scottish railways were earliest to adopt the 4-4-0. The first to appear were built by Cowan for the GNoSR between 1862 and 1866. These were outside-cylinder engines, and some lasted into the 1920s.

From that time onwards, the GNoSR built nothing but 4-4-0s so far as tender engines were concerned. From 1884 onwards they were all inside-cylinder machines of the same general design, built under the respective superintendencies of W. Cowan, J. Manson, J. Johnson, W. Pickersgill and T. Heywood. A Johnson engine of 1893 was photographed at Fraserburgh in 1949, three years before it was scrapped (**148**).

150 Most Scottish 4-4-0s had inside cylinders, a trend pioneered by two built by Wheatley at Cowlairs in 1871 for the North British, with 6ft 6in driving wheels and 17×24in cylinders. One of these, No 224, achieved fame in being the unfortunate engine which went down into the

150

151

152

153

river in the Tay Bridge disaster of December 1879. It was later salvaged and repaired, to give many years of service until withdrawn in 1919.

151 These engines were followed by three handsome 4-4-0s built by Dugald Drummond in 1876, one of which was No 476 *Abbotsford*. They were the forerunners of similar engines designed by Drummond for the Caledonian and London & South Western, on which railways he continued his career. His brother, Peter Drummond, produced engines for the Highland Railway with a strong family resemblance, for example No 14404 *Ben Clebrig* (**161**).

152 The best known of the later NBR 4-4-0s built by Reid were the Scotts, with 6ft 6in driving wheels, and the very similar Glen 6ft 0in class. One of the latter, No 256 *Glen Douglas*, was restored to working order in 1959 and worked rail tours for a few years. It is now in Glasgow Museum.

153 James Stirling on the Glasgow & South Western brought out his first 4-4-0s for that railway in 1875. They had 7ft 1in driving wheels with 18 × 26in cylinders, and all survived the grouping to become LMS 14228 to 14243. No 14236 still retained its domeless boiler when photographed in 1927; it was not scrapped until 1930. Others latterly carried domed boilers. Until 1915 these engines were followed by a succession of classes of increasing power designed by Stirling's successors. The later ones had short lives, however, all having been withdrawn by 1937.

James Stirling was to build many very similar engines for the South Eastern Railway, to which he went in 1877. The majority of these lasted into Southern days, mostly rebuilt by Wainwright with domes and extended smokeboxes, and a few even survived into nationalisation. These were of two classes, the smaller ones class F (**154**) and later F1; the larger ones B, later B1 after rebuilding by Wainwright (**155**).

155

154

156

156 Dugald Drummond moved from the North British to the Caledonian Railway in 1882. The railway already had some outside-cylinder 4-4-0s built by Connor and Brittain, but Drummond introduced his own typical inside-cylinder version in 1884. They were followed by some engines built in 1894 by Lambie, which in turn developed into the well-known Dunalastair series introduced by McIntosh in 1896. There were in all four main variations of these with successive enlargements, the Dunalastair I for example No 721 *Dunalastair*, which appeared in 1896, the IIs in 1897–8, the IIIs in 1889 and the Dunalastair IVs between 1904 and 1914.

Pickersgill continued the basic design with a further 48 engines built between 1916 and 1922. In their day the earlier Dunalastairs were among the most advanced engines of their time. From 1910 onwards they were all fitted with superheaters, the first Scottish engines to be so equipped. The size of the driving wheels remained constant at 6ft 6in throughout, but other dimensions were progressively enlarged, the final Pickersgill engines have $20\frac{1}{2} \times 26$in cylinders and 180lb pressure.

Most of the earlier series were scrapped before the war, having become LMS 14311–14365 and 14430–14437; the later ones, BR 54438–54508, nearly all lasted into the 1950s and early 1960s, although for many years they were relegated to secondary duties (**157**).

Bogies. No 14100, photographed at Dundee in 1928, was scrapped in 1930.

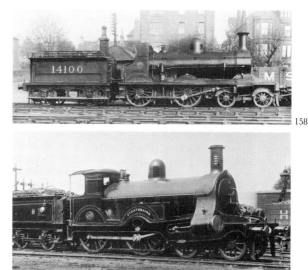
158

157

158 Ten Brittain 4-4-0s were built in 1882 for working the hilly Oban line. They were known as the Oban

159

159 The Highland Railway, under the superintendency of David Jones, built its first 4-4-0s in 1874; by 1892 there were 48 of them, all with outside cylinders, combined by picturesque curves with the smokebox, Allan style. They were of four classes, including the Skye Bogies with 5ft 3in wheels; these were specially built for the Kyle of Lochalsh line with its numerous curves, over which 2-4-0s had been found to have too rigid a wheelbase. The last 12 engines, the Straths, had 6ft 3in wheels and 18 × 24in cylinders. No 93 *Strathnairn* was one of these. Built in 1892 some of them, together with most of the Skye Bogies, survived into LMS days as 14271–14277 and 14279–14285. 14278 was the sole survivor of an earlier class, accidentally renumbered out of order.

160 15 of an improved Loch class were designed by David Jones in 1896, a further three being built in 1917. No 14391 was rebuilt with a Caledonian boiler after the grouping.

160

161

161 Jones' successor, Peter Drummond, who took over in 1896, built a number of 4-4-0s with inside cylinders to his distinctive outlines: the Small Bens such as No 14404 *Ben Clebrig*, and the Large Bens. There were also two large machines with outside cylinders built by F. G. Smith in 1916 for the Far North Road.

162 Returning south, S. W. Johnson, later of Midland fame, built two 4-4-0s for the GER which came out in 1874 after the designer's departure to the MR. These were the first English 4-4-0s with inside cylinders, as distinct from the Scottish ones already described. They had 6ft 7in driving wheels and 17 × 24in cylinders. They were scrapped in 1897-8.

162

163

163 GER No 0704 was one of 11 4-4-0s built by Holden in 1884-5 as two-cylinder compounds. They were later converted to simple engines, and all were withdrawn between 1902 and 1904.

164 Mr William Adams, who was loco superintendent on the GER between 1873 and 1878 before going to the LSWR, produced twenty 4-4-0s. They were in fact reconstructed from 2-4-0s built by one of his predecessors, Robert Sinclair, between 1859 and 1866. They had 6ft 3in driving wheels and 17 × 24in cylinders.

165

164

165 During his 18 years on the LSWR between 1878 and 1895 Adams built several series of 4-4-0s. The first 20 were poor things, and may be disregarded, but the later ones were very fine machines. These consisted of 12 mixed traffic engines with 5ft 7in wheels known as the Steamrollers, followed by five series of express engines with 6ft 7in and 7ft 1in driving wheels, in accordance

with LSWR practice. This lasted into Drummond's days, the larger wheels being intended for the lines east of Salisbury and the smaller ones for use west thereof. There were eventually 54 of the seven footers and 51 of the others, again of two more varieties. A representative of each is illustrated, No 0448, of the earlier 7ft 1in design with Drummond chimney; and No 563 of the later 6ft 7in type as originally built (**166**). This engine has been preserved and can be seen in York Museum.

166

167

168

driving wheels, 18 × 24in cylinders (the earlier ones were 17 × 22in) and 160lb pressure. Many later received Belpaire fireboxes and superheaters, and lasted until the 1950s. No 57 was photographed in 1934 in original condition showing the very unusual double-hinged type of smokebox door. There was also a smaller version with 5ft 8½in wheels.

168 Johnson's term of office on the Midland Railway lasted for 30 years from 1873 to 1903, during which time he concentrated on a few standard types, mostly built in large numbers; he was one of the earlier advocates of standardisation. His first 4-4-0s came out in 1876–7, ten engines with 6ft 6in driving wheels and 20 with 7ft 0in, to be followed at intervals to 1901 with more of both varieties. They were of the same basic design, but with progressive enlargement, and there were ultimately 265 in all.

Another 40 of the 6ft 6in variety were supplied to the Midland & Great Northern Joint Railway between 1894 and 1899. No 77 was photographed in 1933 as later rebuilt with Belpaire firebox and extended smokebox (**169**).

167 J. A. F. Aspinall was CME of the Great Southern & Western in Ireland from 1883–6, after which he went to the Lancashire & Yorkshire Railway. He built a number of 4-4-0s on both railways, both very similar in appearance, but the Irish ones lasted very much longer than their successors on the mainland, all of which had gone by 1932.

The GS&W engines, which continued to be built under Aspinall's successor, A. McDonnell, had 6ft 7in

169

Allowing for two scrapped before 1907, the whole MR series became 300 to 562. Although the original 30 were never rebuilt, the later ones were eventually reboilered by Deeley, at first unsuperheated with or without extended smokeboxes and Belpaire fireboxes (**170**). They were ultimately rebuilt by Fowler with superheaters and new frames, virtually new engines (**171**), and forming what was to become LMS standard class 2 after the grouping. 138 of these were constructed between 1928 and 1932, including three for the Somerset & Dorset Joint built at Derby in 1928. All of them had 6ft 9in

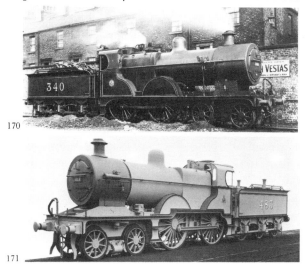

170

171

driving wheels in place of the 7ft 0in ones of the Fowler rebuilds. They were LMS 563–700, Nos 633–635 being the S&DJR engines, which were incorporated into LMS stock in 1930. These engines were to be found in large numbers on the G&SWR, where they very quickly displaced that company's own 4-4-0s. Although the last of these standard class 2 4-4-0s were not withdrawn until 1963, none were set aside for preservation.

172   In 1900, there appeared on the Midland an entirely new class of 4-4-0 with larger boilers and Belpaire fireboxes. They had 6ft 9in driving wheels and $19\frac{1}{2} \times 26$in cylinders, increased to $20\frac{1}{2} \times 26$in on being superheated, as most of them were in later years. They were of somewhat plainer appearance than Johnson's earlier 4-4-0s, but still of handsome proportions. They became Nos 700–779 in 1907, and were classified as power class 3.

They did very good work over the Midland main lines alongside the compounds right up to the grouping, and although superior in many ways to the class 2 Fowlers, they were inclined to be heavy on coal, probably the reason for their not being adopted as a standard LMS type rather than the Fowler design. A few were scrapped in the 1920s without receiving superheaters, but the last one in service was withdrawn in 1952 as LMS 40726.

In 1907 Deeley built ten somewhat similar engines with 6ft 6in wheels for the Leeds and Carlisle line, Nos 990–999. They were scrapped in the late 1920s.

The first four-cylinder main line engines to appear in Great Britain came out almost simultaneously in 1897 on three different railways. Two of them were 4-4-0s and the third its very near equivalent, a 4-(2-2)-0.

172

173

173 The G&SWR was first in the field, with an engine built by James Manson. No 11 was a four-cylinder simple, the cylinders being situated in line with the smokebox. The inside cylinders had a common steam chest, the valves being worked by Stephenson's link motion, which through rocking shafts also operated the valves of the outside cylinders. These latter were 12½ × 24in, and the inside cylinders were 14½ × 26in. The engine had 6ft 9½in driving wheels. No 11 became 394 in 1919 and received the name *Lord Glenarthur*, the only G&SWR engine ever to receive this distinction. Whitelegg rebuilt it in 1923 with piston valves and a very large boiler, as illustrated. As LMS 14509 it was scrapped in 1934.

174 Two months after the appearance of the G&SWR engines came two 4-4-0s on the LNWR, a four-cylinder simple No 1501 *Iron Duke*, and 1502 *Black Prince*, the latter a compound but very different from Webb's previous efforts in this direction. Not only were four cylinders used in place of three, but also the driving wheels were coupled. A leading bogie was fitted, these two engines being the first products of Crewe to be so equipped. There were ultimately 80 of these four-cylinder compounds, but most of them were eventually rebuilt as two-cylinder simples, and even these had all gone by 1931. No 1955 *Hannibal* (illustrated), was scrapped in 1923 without being rebuilt.

174

175 It was curious that Webb's abandonment of the non-coupled engine, hitherto his exclusive prerogative, should coincide with its adoption by another locomotive superintendent at a time when each was responsible for the introduction of four-cylinder engines. Dugald Drummond, already mentioned in connection with his 4-4-0s on the North British and Caledonian, had just succeeded Adams on the London & South Western. His first express engine for this line was a four-cylinder 'double single' on the general lines of Webb's compounds, but in this case a 4-(2-2)-0 and with simple propulsion. The first one, No 720, came out from Nine Elms in 1897. His idea was to combine the advantages of the free running single-wheeler, uncluttered by coupling rods, with increased adhesion of the coupled engine. The theory did not work out in practice, and pairs of uncoupled driving wheels were never again tried by any other locomotive designer.

The four cylinders were 15 × 26in, the inside ones driving the front pair of wheels, and the outside ones the rear. The driving wheels were 6ft 7in in diameter. No 720 was at first fitted with a 4ft 7in boiler, but in 1903 it was fitted with a larger 5ft 0in one. It was photographed in this form at Nine Elms in 1921. Meanwhile five more of the type had been built in 1901, Nos 369–373, but these were never similarly modified. The firebox water tubes were however later removed.

These double singles were not very popular and were used only in times of busy traffic or in emergencies. All six were scrapped in 1926, but two survived long enough to be repainted in SR style as Nos E372 and E373 (**176**).

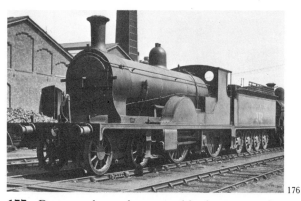

176

177 Drummond was also engaged in the perpetuation of what could be called his standard 4-4-0 design already seen on the North British and Caledonian railways. The first of this type for the LSWR, the 290 class, came out in 1898. They were followed by an improved version with a longer coupled wheelbase and larger firebox, the T9 class. This was later to become well regarded as an extremely successful design, particularly after superheating. Many of these engines remained in service right though to the 1960s.

No 120 has been preserved, in its rebuilt form, and is now in York Museum, but the illustration shows No 714 in original condition. The panel at the rear end of the boiler housed Drummond's patent arrangement of firebox water tubes which he applied to all of his express engines, but which were later removed by his successor Urie.

175

177

No 286, photographed at Eastleigh in 1947 in rebuilt form, was temporarily converted to oil burning to cope with the coal crisis of that year (**178**).

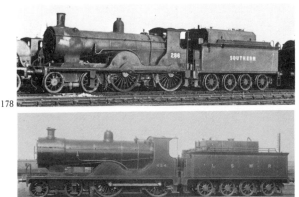
178

179

179 The T9s were followed by other larger designs of 4-4-0s, good enough engines, but never to attain the fame of the T9s. No 424, an example of the later ones, underwent a temporary conversion to oil burning during the 1921 coal strike.

180 Among Wilson Worsdell's several classes of 4-4-0 for the North Eastern Railway, many of them first built as Worsdell von Borries two-cylinder compounds, were two engines built in 1896, Nos 1869 and 1870. They had 7ft 7in driving wheels, the largest coupled wheels ever seen in the British Isles. They were built primarily as racing engines, probably in anticipation of a continuation of the competition between the east and west coast routes of 1888 and 1895, which however was not repeated. They were scrapped in 1930. Another similar engine, with 7ft 1¾in wheels, No 1621, which actually took part in the 1895 race, is preserved in York Museum.

180

181 In 1899 Worsdell designed some very handsome 4-4-0s, of which 60 were built up to 1907. All were later superheated, and most remained in service into British Railways days, the last being withdrawn in 1956.

182 In 1900 the famous *Claud Hamilton* appeared on the Great Eastern. Designed by Holden, it was in the opinion of many one of the most handsome of all British locomotives, with its rich royal blue livery, red and yellow lining and elaborate brass work. Such claims could well be made for many other 4-4-0 designs, a type which seemed to lend itself so easily to the production of a pleasing outline. *Claud Hamilton* was numbered after

the year of its birth, and was followed in succession by batches of ten in reverse order, 1890–1899, 1880–1889, and so on, back to LNER E1780–E1789, which came out after the grouping. They subsequently had Belpaire fireboxes, but they underwent various rebuildings in later years, especially under Gresley after the grouping, resulting in the disappearance of the elaborate framing, the beautiful copper-capped chimney and other features. He also substituted round-topped fireboxes in place of Belpaires, which he always disliked. They had 7ft 0in driving wheels, and 19 × 26in cylinders. The last of them was scrapped in 1960, regrettably none surviving for preservation.

The Great Western was not a particularly large user of 4-4-0s, at least on main line express work. The type had a fairly short reign, being largely displaced by 4-6-0s in the first few years of the century. Their history is nevertheless a very complicated one, difficult to summarise.

183 The first engines of the type, designed by William Dean, appeared in 1894; four 7ft 1in engines No 7 *Armstrong*, 8 *Gooch*, 14 *Charles Saunders* and 16 *Brunel*. They were later incorporated into the Flower class as Nos 4169–4172.

These engines were followed by the Duke of Cornwall class in 1895, equipped with 5ft 8in wheels to cope principally with the hilly lines west of Newton Abbot. There were originally 60 of these, built up to 1899. Next came the Camels and Bulldogs up to 1910, all mixed traffic engines, classification being complicated by numerous variations in boilers and fittings, and a good deal of renumbering and renaming. There were eventually 196 engines in all.

183

185

What may be termed the express engines with 6ft 8in wheels comprised the Badminton class, which came out in 1897, the first GWR engines to have Belpaire fireboxes; and the Atbaras, Cities and finally the Flowers in 1908, 90 engines altogether. All these had double frames.

184 The only outside-cylinder 4-4-0s of typical Churchward design were the 40 Counties of 1904–12. These had the standard 6ft 8in wheels and 18 × 30in cylinders. All disappeared in the early 1930s, as by that time the GWR had no use for four-coupled engines on main line express duties.

184

185 The rest of the 4-4-0s continued to work secondary and cross-country services and in fact a new class for such duties was created in 1936 by the rebuilding of 29 of the curved framed Dukes; mounting their boilers and cabs on to the straight frames of an equal number of the more modern Bulldogs. These inevitably became known as the 'Dukedogs' and were at first named after Earls, but these names were later removed.

Built as 3200–3228, these engines later became 9000–9028 and together with about 35 of the original Bulldogs they were the only GWR 4-4-0s to survive into the nationalisation period. They worked mainly on the Cambrian section. One of them, restored as No 3217 *Earl of Berkeley*, can be seen on the Bluebell Railway.

No 3204 *Earl of Dartmouth* was photographed as turned out from Swindon in 1936, being in fact a reconstruction of No 3271 *Eddystone* and 3439 *Weston-super-Mare*.

186 The most famous of all GWR 4-4-0s was No 3440 *City of Truro*, reputed to have attained a speed of 102.3

mph in 1904. Some criticism has been made in recent years of the accuracy of this recording, but there is little doubt that something very like 100 mph was recorded on this historic occasion.

On withdrawal in 1931 it was placed in York Museum, where it remained until 1957. It was then restored to running order, mainly for working enthusiasts' specials, but also working in ordinary service. The engine is now in Swindon museum.

186

187   It was not until the appearance of Whale's Precursors in 1904 that the LNWR had a reliable express engine capable of working the increasing loads of the main line passenger trains. True, Webb's Precedent 2-4-0s had performed wonders considering their size, but were considerably underpowered for such duties and generally had to be used in pairs or double heading the notorious 3-cylinder compounds. The latter very soon went to the scrap heap after the appearance of the new engines. There were 130 Precursors, built in 1904–1907. They had 6ft 9in driving wheels, 19 × 26in cylinders and 175lb pressure.

187

188   Bowen Cooke, Whale's successor, introduced a superheated version in 1910, the George the Fifth class. The cylinders were increased to 20½ × 26in. Ten of the original 20, the Queen Mary class, were originally turned out without superheaters for comparison purposes, but very soon received them as did most of the Precursors, and in later years many of them also received Belpaire fireboxes. The number of George the Fifths had

188

reached 90 by 1915. These engines in particular did very fine work on the LNWR main lines for many years, at very high average speeds for the time. They could well rank among the best of all 4-4-0s for performance.

The unsuperheated Precursors became LMS 5187–5266 at the grouping, the superheated ones 5270–5319, and the George the Fifths 5320–5409. A handful lasted to 1948, but not long enough to receive BR numbers. The illustration shows George the Fifth No 2494, *Perseus*, later LMS 5368, scrapped 1934.

189 Charles Sacré's 4-4-0s for the MS&LR were double framed with 6ft 3in driving wheels, consisting of 27 engines built between 1877 and 1880. 12 survived the grouping, one of the last being LNER 6466, photographed as GCR No 440 in 1926.

Sacré's successors on the MS&LR, Parker and Pollitt, produced a large number of handsome engines with inside cylinders, which were to be found until the 1930s on cross-country services in Lincolnshire.

190 On the GCR Robinson built some very fine 4-4-0s. The earlier ones of 1901–4, 40 in all, were handsome engines as usual with all the products of this locomotive engineer, with sweeping splashers similar to those on Wainwright's D class SE&CR engines. They had 6ft 9in wheels, with $18\frac{1}{2} \times 26$in cylinders. In later years they were fitted with large boilers and superheated, as shown in the 1926 photograph of LNER 6016. Although displaced from London expresses in their early years by the Atlantics, most lasted until nationalisation, the final survivors finishing their days on the fast expresses on the Cheshire Lines road between Manchester and Liverpool up to 1950.

189

190

191 The Director class of 1913 were somewhat different in appearance with straight combined splashers over smaller ones accommodating the coupling rods, which were later cut away with raised framing to give access for lubrication. There were ten of these engines, followed by another 11 of a slightly different enlarged version in 1920–22. One of these, No 5502 *Zeebrugge*, was photographed at Neasden in 1925. Another, No 506 *Butler Henderson*, has been preserved, one of the only two

191

192

Great Central engines still in existence, and can be seen at the Great Central Main Line Steam Trust at Loughboro'.

After the grouping Gresley built another 24 of the same design, specially for use north of the border, with appropriate Scottish names. All of the later Directors were scrapped between 1959 and 1961, the original ten having already been taken out of service in the earlier 1950s.

192 The second major railway which can definitely be described as a 4-4-0 line, the other of course being the Midland, was the SE&CR, on which it likewise remained the principal express type up to the grouping. Apart from a large fleet inherited from the SER and a sizeable contingent from the LC&DR, Wainwright introduced his own engines in 1901. This was another design which could take a very high place among the contestants for the title of the most handsome locomotive. Even shorn of their original embellishments they could still qualify for such distinction in Southern days, as seen in the photograph of No 1501, taken in 1937.

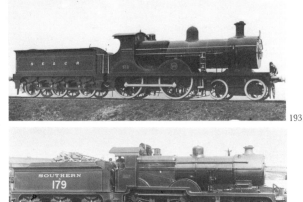

193

194

There were 51 of these engines, known as class D, built from 1901 to 1907, and another 26 of a Belpaire version with extended smokebox, Class E, built from 1905 to 1909 (**193**). Maunsell completely modernised a number of both classes with superheaters and piston valves, 32 in all redesignated classes D1 and E1 (**194**); in their new form they very much resembled the Midland Fowler class 2s. These engines had 6ft 8in driving wheels, 19 × 28in cylinders, and 180lb pressure.

All the unrebuilt engines had been withdrawn by 1956, but one of them, No 737, restored to its former glory, can be seen in York Museum. The rebuilt D1s and E1s lasted into nationalisation, nearly all until the early 1960s. Other early additions to the fleet of SE&CR 4-4-0s were five engines of pure GNoSR design purchased in 1905 to meet an acute engine shortage; these were at work until the mid 1920s.

195 Wainwright prepared the drawings for a new enlarged type of 4-4-0, class L, in 1913, but they did not appear until 1914, after his retirement. 12 were built by Beyer Peacock, Nos 760–771, and another ten, Nos 772–781, were built abroad by A. Borsig of Berlin; it was an almost unique event for a British railway to order engines from overseas. They were delivered shortly before the outbreak of war. These engines had the usual 6ft 8in driving wheels, and 20 × 26in cylinders. The name *Betty Baldwin* on No 763 was unofficial, being applied by volunteers during the 1926 general strike. It was soon removed as being against official policy at the time.

The final version of SE&CR 4-4-0 design did not appear until 1926 after the grouping – the class L1, Nos A753–A759 and A782–A789 (**196**). In appearance they

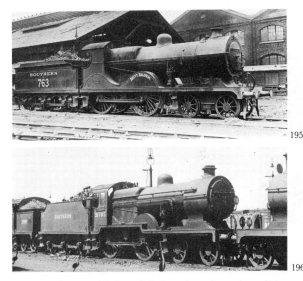

195

196

very much resembled a slightly enlarged version of the rebuilt D1s and E1s, and like them and their immediate predecessors lasted into the late 1950s and early 1960s.

Before dealing with what may be termed the final generation of 4-4-0s, brief mention must be made of some of the engines to be found on the remaining railways to use the type.

197 On some railways 4-4-0s had only a short transitional reign between 2-4-0s and single-wheelers to Atlantics or 4-6-0s. One such line was the Great Northern,

197

where Ivatt built quite a number, but they were quickly relegated to use on secondary services. No 3400 (built 1896) is a typical example.

198 L&YR No 1099, which had surprisingly large 7ft 3in driving wheels, was designed by J. A. F. Aspinall, and built in 1891. Allocated LMS No 10155, it was scrapped in 1928 without carrying it.

198

199 Billinton produced several designs of 4-4-0 for the LB&SCR, one of which is represented by No 54 *Tasmania*, built in 1900 and later renamed *Princess Royal*. This design presented a delightful study in curves.

200 A typical 4-4-0 of the Cambrian Railway, No 60 was built in 1891. It became GWR 1112 and was scrapped in 1928.

199

200

201

202

203

201 LMS (NCC) No 87 *Queen Alexandra* was a rebuild of a two-cylinder compound built at Derby in 1905, reconstructed in 1936 on typical Midland lines. There were 18 of these Castle class engines, most of them built new to the design in 1924 and 1925. One is preserved in Belfast Museum, No 74 *Dunluce Castle*.

202 William Kirtley designed a series of 44 4-4-0s for the London Chatham & Dover Railway, which were built between 1877 and 1900. Absorbed into the SE&CR in 1900, several of them were still in service at the grouping, the last one being scrapped in 1928.

203 Five North Stafford 4-4-0s were absorbed into the LMS at the grouping. They became Nos 595–599 in the LMS list, and the last one was withdrawn in 1933.

204 The Furness had twenty 4-4-0s at the grouping, of several classes, all scrapped by 1932. No 126 was one of four built in 1900–1 by Messrs Sharp Stewart & Co.

204

205 Five 4-4-0s were built by Matthew Stirling in 1910 for the Hull & Barnsley Railway. They were all fitted with typical Stirling domeless boilers.

206 The Midland and South Western Junction Railway (Absorbed by the Great Western Railway in 1923) had nine 4-4-0s, built between 1905 and 1914. Most of them were eventually rebuilt at Swindon with taper boilers, but the last of them was withdrawn in 1938.

207

205

208

206

207 S&DJR engines were in later years of Derby design, although not necessarily identical with those of the parent company. No 77 was one of a handsome pair built by Deeley in 1908.

208 Possibly the finest 4-4-0s ever to appear were Maunsell's Schools class, his last design of passenger engine and regarded by many as his best. They were built to satisfy the need for a locomotive with approximately the same haulage capacity as the very successful King Arthur 4-6-0s, but with greater route availability, particularly for use on the Hastings line of the SE&CR. The new engines were in some ways a 4-4-0 version of the Lord Nelsons, but with two important differences, the use of three cylinders in place of four, and the fitting of a round-topped firebox instead of a Belpaire. They had 6ft 7in driving wheels, three 16½ × 26in cylinders and 220lb pressure. 40 came out between 1930 and 1935, numbered 900–939, by coincidence the same numbers as the final batch of LMS compounds, and they were named after public schools. All were in service until the early 1960s. Three have been preserved, No 925 *Cheltenham*, officially by BR, destined for the NRM at York, 928 *Stowe* on the East Somerset Railway at Cranmore and 926 *Repton* in the USA.

209 Prior to the Schools, which was the last new design of 4-4-0 in Great Britain (but not in Ireland) Gresley had built a fleet of three-cylinder engines for intermediate express work on the North Eastern and North British sections of the LNER. Most of the Shires had Walschaert's valve gear with slide valves and the Hunts had Lentz rotary cam poppet valves. All had 6ft 8in wheels, three 17 × 26in cylinders and 180lb pressure. No 318 *Cambridgeshire* was one of six which had a combination of Walschaert's valve gear and Lentz oscillating cam poppet valves. There were 76 engines in all, built between 1927 and 1937, eventually to become BR 62700–62775. The last of them was withdrawn in 1961. No 246 *Morayshire* is preserved at the premises of the Scottish Railway Preservation Society at Falkirk.

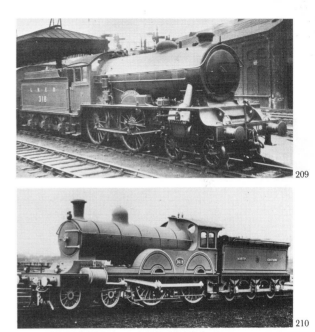

209

210

210 The origins of the famous Midland compounds go back to an experimental engine on the North Eastern, a Worsdell von Borries two-cylinder compound of 1893 which was rebuilt in 1898 as a three-cylinder balanced compound on a system patented by one W. M. Smith. As rebuilt No 1619 had two outside low-pressure 20 × 24in cylinders, and one 19 × 26in high-pressure cylinder between the frames and below the smokebox. It was designed to work either as compound, semi-compound or simple, by means of a complicated system of regulating and reducing valves whereby high-pressure steam could be admitted, partly or directly to the low pressure cylinders. This was of considerable advantage when starting a heavy train.

211 Johnson used the same system with his new engines, five of which were built in 1902–3, Nos 2631–2635. They had two 21 × 26in low-pressure cylinders and a single high-pressure cylinder, 7ft 0in driving wheels and 195lb pressure.

211

212 In 1905 Deeley modified the Johnson design. The Smith-type valves were done away with and replaced by a simpler system under which the high-pressure steam could be admitted directly to the low-pressure steam-chest when required. The boiler pressure was raised to 220lb and the appearance of the new engines, Nos 1000–1029, was noticeably different from that of their predecessors. The original Johnson engines were later

modified to conform, and including these the Deeley design by 1909 totalled 45 engines, Nos 1000–1044, all being eventually superheated. No more were built in Midland days, but the design was adopted by the LMS as a standard type, with a further 195 engines being turned out by Fowler between 1924 and 1932, Nos 1045–1199, and 900–939. The dimensions remained the same as the original Deeleys except for the substitution of 6ft 9in driving wheels and 200lb pressure. The class as a whole did magnificent work, not only on the parent system but also on the Caledonian and G&SWR main lines, and on the LNWR Birmingham two-hour expresses, for which they were ideally suited. They were however not in general popular on that railway, probably owing to a mistrust of compound engines in general dating back to Webb days.

No 1054 made history by running non-stop from Euston to Edinburgh, nearly 400 miles, in May 1928, with a specially adapted tender to increase the coal capacity. The engine, equipped with the special tender, was later photographed on a Birmingham train. This was the LMS's quiet answer to the much publicised inauguration of non-stop running over the east coast route, involving the use of a corridor tender to enable the footplate crew to be relieved en route. At the same time the Glasgow portion of the *Royal Scot*, divided into two trains for this special event, was worked similarly non-stop behind one of the new Royal Scot engines, No 6113.

Lowering standards of maintenance during and after World War Two, to which the compounds were particularly susceptible, led to their falling into some disrepute through no fault of their own, as they were splendid engines when well maintained and properly handled. All

212

213

214 The Great Northern of Ireland was another railway which remained faithful to the 4-4-0 to the end, the chief reason in this case being the limitation imposed by the length of the traversers in Dundalk works, which could not accommodate a larger engine.

There were several classes built by Glover and his predecessor of which No 174 *Carrantuohill*, built in 1913, is an example. No 171 *Slieve Gallion*, of this class, is preserved in working order by the R.P.S.I.

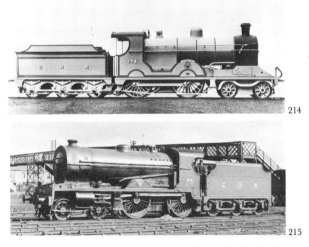

214

215

passed into nationalisation, but withdrawals started in 1948 and by 1959 less than a dozen remained. The original No 1000 has been preserved in working order, and is sometimes used on steam specials (**213**). It is normally to be seen in York Museum.

215 In 1932 five very fine compounds were built for the newly inaugurated *Enterprise* express between Belfast and

Dublin, with accelerated timings. They had 250lb boiler pressure, 6ft 7in driving wheels, and the cylinders consisted of one inside high-pressure 17¼ × 26in, and two low-pressure outside 19 × 26in. They shared a number of features in common with the LMS compounds, though not their appearance. Originally fitted with round-topped fireboxes, Belpaires were later substituted. They were named after birds, No 83 *Eagle*, 84 *Falcon*, 85 *Merlin*, 86 *Peregrine*, and 87 *Kestrel*. *Merlin* is preserved at Belfast, and is currently being restored to working order.

216 In 1948 a further five somewhat similar engines appeared, designed by H. McIntosh for the *Enterprise* service, but in this case with three-cylinder simple propulsion. The cylinders were 15¼ × 26in, and the other dimensions were much as the compounds. These engines were named after rivers, No 206 *Liffey*, 207 *Boyne*, 208 *Lagan*, 209 *Foyle*, and 210 *Erne*. They had fairly short lives, as steam working virtually ceased in the early 1960s. It was the last new design of 4-4-0 in the British Isles, probably in the whole world.

217

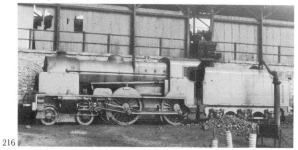

216

217 Concurrently with these new main line engines it was decided to obtain five more 4-4-0s of a 1915 design by Glover for cross-country work, a curious throw-back almost to the Edwardian era. The only modern touch was in the pattern of the cab and tender. They were neat little engines, as can be seen by the photograph of No 204 *Antrim*. They were Nos 201–205, respectively *Meath*, *Louth*, *Armagh*, *Antrim* and *Down*, following on the original Nos 196–200 which were also updated by being given the names *Lough Gill*, *Lough Neagh*, *Lough Swilly*, *Lough Derg* and *Lough Melvin*, and the new blue livery. They had 5ft 9in driving wheels, and 18 × 24in cylinders.

Which of these two series (the Rivers and the Counties) can rightly be regarded as the last 4-4-0s ever to be built is problematical, as both classes came out at about the same time from the firm of Beyer Peacock & Co., who had supplied many engines for the GNR over the years. The Rivers carried building plates dated 1948 with works numbers 6961–6965, whereas the small engines were dated 1947, but with makers' list numbers 7244–7248.

218

4-4-0T

218 The 4-4-0T was very largely a type peculiar to the Metropolis, and it had first appeared in 1855 on the North London. This railway adopted it as its standard passenger engine throughout its independent existence. Although it was nominally absorbed by the LNWR in 1909, the North London did in practice retain much of its separate identity from an operational standpoint right up to the grouping.

Its second design of 4-4-0T, built by William Adams at the railway's works at Bow between 1863 and 1869, had inside cylinders; but better known in later years were those of J. C. Park's design, who replaced Adams as CME in 1873. These had outside cylinders allied by sweeping curves to the smokebox, Allan style, and they worked the whole of the North London passenger services up to the grouping in 1923, by which time there remained 77 of them. Many of these were classified as 'renewals', but they were virtually new engines of the same design, a process which had continued up to 1910.

The LMS were fairly quick to replace them with more modern types, at first Jinty 0-6-0Ts and later 2-6-2Ts, and all had been withdrawn by 1929. The last survivor, as LMS 6445, was set aside for preservation, but was unfortunately broken up in 1932.

219 The 4-4-0T was also for many years the sole wheel arrangement in use on the Metropolitan Railway, and on the Metropolitan District Railway (an entirely separate concern). 18 engines were delivered to the former by Messrs Beyer Peacock & Co in 1864, and 24 to the Metropolitan District in 1871. Ultimately there were 66 on the Metropolitan, delivered up to 1885, and 54 on the District, the last coming out in 1886. An important feature was the condensing apparatus for use in the tunnels. The exhaust steam was diverted from the blast pipe in the smokebox to the top of the side tanks, where it was discharged into the water.

The majority of these engines were scrapped when the lines were electrified in 1905, but a few were retained for

219

departmental and other duties, including the working of the Metropolitan Brill branch until closure in 1935. Quite a number of others were sold to various railways and collieries; two which went to the Cambrian were rebuilt as 4-4-0 tender engines.

The last survivor, No 23, has been restored by the London Transport Board in its original condition, and can be seen at the LT museum being established at the time of writing at Covent Garden. The engines had 5ft 9in wheels and 17 × 24in cylinders. 28 further engines of the same general type were also built by Messrs Beyer Peacock for the Midland, LNWR and LSWR.

220 As far remote from London as can be, the Highland had three 4-4-0Ts, dating back to 1878–9, of such similarity to the NLR engines that one is illustrated here for the sake of comparison. They became LMS 15010 to 15012, and disappeared between 1928 and 1932.

221

220

221 The 4-4-0T had in fact much earlier origins in the form of a number of broad gauge saddle tanks which W. F. Gooch (brother of Daniel Gooch) had built for the South Devon Railway. The first of these dated back to 1851; they had 5ft 8in driving wheels and 17 × 24in cylinders. There had been others of very similar design on the Bristol & Exeter and the Vale of Neath Railways. The South Devon Railway was absorbed by the GWR in 1876, and *Gorgon*, one of a batch built in 1866, became GWR 2122. It worked until the end of the 7ft 0in gauge in 1892.

222 Dugald Drummond built 30 4-4-0Ts for the North British between 1880 and 1884 with 5ft 0in wheels for branch line and local suburban work around Edinburgh and Glasgow. Together with three larger engines with 6ft 0in wheels, all of these survived the grouping, although they had been withdrawn by 1933. One of their last duties was on the former GNoSR St Combs branch, which, being unfenced, accounts for the cowcatcher fitted to No 10456, photographed in 1930.

222

4ft 6in wheels and 15 × 20in cylinders. Several worked at Government Depots during World War One, and one was still to be seen on the Longmoor Military Railway until 1952.

224 4-4-0Ts were the principal type in use on three of the Irish 3ft 0in gauge lines. They accounted for eight of the Cavan & Leitrim's stock of nine engines (this was before the importation of 2-4-2Ts from the Cork Black-rock & Passage under GSR auspices). Built in 1884, No 4 *Violet* had 3ft 6in driving wheels and 14 × 20in cylinders. No 2 *Kathleen* is preserved in Belfast Museum and No 3 *Lady Edith* is in the USA.

223 A small class of charming 4-4-0Ts to be found on the Midland & Great Northern Joint Railway, were originally built in 1878–1880 for the Lynn & Fakenham and the Yarmouth & North Norfolk Railways. They had

224

223

On the Cork & Muskerry six out of the eight engines were likewise 4-4-0Ts, as were the three later engines of the Schull & Skibbereen: No 3 *Kent* (**225**) was built in 1914 and scrapped in 1934.

4-4-2

The 4-4-2, or Atlantic type as it was generally known, the

225

design having originated in the USA, enjoyed a fairly brief spell of popularity during the earlier years of the century. It was in the nature of a bridge between the 4-4-0, which had become established as the principal locomotive type for main line express work, and the 4-6-0, which was to become standard on most of the larger companies before finally giving way in its turn to the 4-6-2 Pacific.

226 The first British Atlantic was designed by H. A. Ivatt for the Great Northern in 1898. The original engine, No 990, was later named *Henry Oakley* (the only GNR engine ever to receive a name until the first Pacific *Great Northern* appeared in 1922, just before the grouping). It was followed by ten others in 1900 and a final ten in 1903. They had 6ft 7½in driving wheels with two outside cylinders, 18¾ × 24in. *Henry Oakley* is preserved

at York. In 1902 a similar engine was produced, but with four 15 × 20in cylinders. It was later rebuilt with two inside cylinders — the only one of its type (**227**).

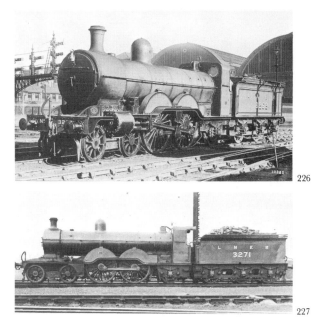

226

227

228 A much larger version appeared in 1902, the main feature being the wide firebox extending sideways over the trailing wheels, not possible with 4-4-0 or 4-6-0. The increased grate area contributed in no small measure to the success of these engines, although the idea was not followed up by any other subsequent designer of such locomotives. The use of a large boiler resulted in an exceedingly impressive locomotive for its time.

Eventually there were 94 of these engines, known as the Large Atlantics as distinct from their smaller predecessors. Four of them ran for a time as four-cylinder compounds, and in later years one was fitted with an auxiliary pair of cylinders to the trailing wheels, for assistance in starting a heavy train, known as a booster. They remained the staple express engine on the GNR main line right up to the grouping. No 251 has been preserved and can be seen in the NRM at York.

228

229 D. Earle Marsh, who had served at Doncaster before becoming CME of the LB&SCR, built some almost identical engines for that railway, five in 1905–6 and another six in 1911. One of the latter, BR No 32424 *Beachy Head* ran until 1958, by which time it was the last Atlantic in ordinary service.

229

230 In 1899 a class of 4-4-2s appeared on the Lancashire & Yorkshire designed by Sir John Aspinall. They were distinctive engines, with 19 × 26in inside cylinders, Joy's valve gear and large 7ft 3in coupled wheels which earned them the nickname 'Highflyers'. There were in all 40 of them, and some of them were initially fitted with a form of steam dryer, an early version of the superheater, this was the first application in this country of what was to become standard practice on the main line designs of later years. The last of the L&YR 4-4-2s went in 1934.

230

231

232

The other railways, not so far mentioned, to employ Atlantics were the NER, NBR, and GCR, and it is a curious fact that of the 295 engines of the type existing at the time of the grouping, no less than 241 of them were on railways which came into the LNER group. The North Eastern had 72, of three classes, the North British 22, and the Great Central 31. It is interesting to note that in the 1920s a journey from Kings Cross to Aberdeen – the east coast route, as it was generally known, would probably involve travel behind Atlantic engines of three companies, the GNR, NER and NBR. The GNR and NBR used them right through to the grouping, and never went over to the 4-6-0.

233 The North Eastern contingent consisted of 20 two-cylinder engines by Worsdell, built between 1903 and 1910 (illustrated), two four-cylinder compounds of 1906, and 50 of Raven's three-cylinder variety.

The latter were very fine engines, and bore the brunt of main line working over the NER for a good many years. Two of them were eventually modernised with high running plates, together with a four-wheeled

231 The Great Western at this time was undecided between the respective merits of the 4-4-2 and the 4-6-0; indeed experiments were made by Churchward with both types concurrently, but the engines running in the Atlantic version were eventually rebuilt as 4-6-0s. At the same time, three four-cylinder de Glehn compounds were imported from France. These ran for several years, later fitted with Swindon taper boilers, and were withdrawn between 1926 and 1928 (**232**).

233

234

booster articulated to the tender, when they might conceivably have been classified as 4-4-4s; if so they would be unique in being the only tender engines in Britain with such a wheel arrangement (**234**).

235 The North British engines were very massive machines with large boilers, 22 engines built between 1906 and 1921; the final one was the last new Atlantic to be constructed for use in Great Britain. They had two outside cylinders of 20×28in, 6ft 9in driving wheels, and were the heaviest of all British Atlantics. The last survivor was No 9875 *Midlothian*, withdrawn in 1939 with plans for preservation, unfortunately thwarted by the war.

235

236 The Great Central engines were possibly the most handsome of all British Atlantics. They were the work of J. G. Robinson, and were built between 1903 and 1906. 27 two-cylinder $19\frac{1}{2} \times 26$in examples were constructed (one engine ran for a time as a three-cylinder simple, 16×26in, with Walschaert's valve gear); there were also four three-cylinder compounds on the Smith system, similar to that on the Midland engines, with one 19×26in high-pressure inside cylinder and two 21×26in low-pressure outside cylinders; all had 6ft 8in driving wheels. Both series had the same outward appearance, except that the compounds were given names, and there seems to have been little difference in performance. Most survived into the nationalisation era, but none later than 1950.

236

4-4-2T

237 The 4-4-2T, sometimes loosely referred to as the Atlantic tank, was first introduced in the British Isles by

237

the London Tilbury & Southend Railway in 1880, which adopted the type exclusively for its busy passenger service until it was absorbed by the Midland in 1912. By that time there were 70 of them, of three distinct stages of development. The locomotive superintendency of the LT&SR was in the hands of T. Whitelegg until 1910; he was succeeded by his son R. H. Whitelegg, who went to the G&SWR in 1918. Although no more were actually built by the Midland, the class was revived by the LMS after the grouping by the construction of further examples between 1923 and 1930, another 35 in all (**238**).

238

They were extremely handsome locomotives, and in fact this applied to most designs of 4-4-2T, as the type seemed to lend itself well to a good looking engine.

In LT&SR days the engines all bore names with a pleasing green livery, but this was replaced under the MR regime with its well-known crimson lake, and the names disappeared. The LMS-built engines of course came out in the style of that company, the earlier ones in maroon and the later ones black. All were scrapped by 1960, but one of the last-built LT&S engines, which came out in 1909, has been preserved and restored as No 80, *Thundersley*; it is now to be seen at Bressingham Hall museum.

With one exception the LMS engines were the last 4-4-2Ts to be built in the British Isles, and were a direct development of the original engine of 1880. The earliest lot had 6ft 1in driving wheels and 17 × 26in cylinders, these and other dimensions being progressively increased through the intermediate stages to 6ft 6in wheels and 19 × 26in cylinders in the later ones.

239 William Adams introduced the type to the LSWR in 1882. These engines had very small side tanks, most of the water being carried in the lower part of the bunker. The tanks were slightly enlarged in the later engines, increasing the water capacity from 1000 to 1200 gallons. There were also 12 engines with normal-size side tanks which were rebuilds of 4-4-0Ts originally built in 1878–9. In all 71 of the later main series were built up to 1885. They had 5ft 7in driving wheels and 17½ × 24in cylinders, and did most of the work on the LSWR suburban services until their gradual replacement by 0-4-4Ts, and eventually by electrification in 1915.

239

In the early 1920s there were a large number of them in Eastleigh yard awaiting scrapping, many of them having lain there for some years. Only about a dozen survived the grouping in actual working order. In 1961 there were still three survivors, specially retained for working the Lyme Regis branch, one of which had meanwhile been sold to the East Kent Railway, but re-purchased by the SR in 1946. This engine, restored as LSWR 488, can now be seen at work on the Bluebell Railway.

240 The first inside-cylinder 4-4-2Ts appeared on the Taff Vale Railway, three engines built in 1888. Thereafter most of the type subsequently to appear on other railways also had inside cylinders.

241 An exception to this rule appeared on the GWR. Churchward built 30 engines for the London suburban services between 1905 and 1912, Nos 2221–2250, together with a solitary smaller version in 1913, No 4600, which was never multiplied. These were among the most modern-looking 4-4-2Ts, although by no means the last

to be built, as the GWR at that period was somewhat in advance of its time. They came to a comparatively early demise in the 1930s, as the Great Western took an early dislike of four-coupled engines for main line semi-express work. No 2221 was photographed at Reading in 1933 after withdrawal.

240

241

242

242 The first really significant application of super-heating was to Earle Marsh's very fine 4-4-2Ts which he introduced to the LB&SCR in 1908. The principles of the Schmidt apparatus, situated in the smokebox, were followed in the ensuing years by other designs developed by Robinson on the GCR, Churchward at Swindon, Gresley, Maunsell, Urie, and others. The Brighton class I3 4-4-2Ts, which had 6ft 7½in driving wheels and 21 × 26in cylinders, were express engines in every sense, their limited water capacity being no handicap over the relatively short main lines of the LB&SCR.

They showed up particularly well in comparison with a LNWR unsuperheated Precursor 4-4-0 during trials in 1909. Both companies worked the *Sunny South Special* throughout between East Croydon and Rugby, a distance of 90½ miles, without taking water, a task which the superheated 4-4-2T managed with ease. Economy in coal consumption was also very marked, and these trials undoubtedly had a strong influence on the adoption of superheating for express work on other railways.

243 Among other designs which demonstrated the generally handsome outlines of the 4-4-2T were the GNR Ivatts of 1898–1907. Most of these 60 engines spent their earlier years on the GNR suburban services until displaced by Gresley's larger N2 class 0-6-2Ts from 1920 onwards. The survivors became BR 67350–67399, the last in service going in 1958.

244 Whale's suburban tanks of 1906–9, built for the London & North Western, numbered 50 engines in all, LMS 6780–6829. They had all gone by 1939.

243

244

245 Robinson on the GCR could always be relied upon to produce a handsome locomotive, and his 4-4-2Ts were no exception. 52 engines were built between 1903 and 1907. They became BR 67400–67451, and all were scrapped by 1960. In their later years their appearance was sadly ruined by the fitting of ugly 'flower pot' type chimneys.

245

246

246 Three 4-4-2Ts were built for the Midland & Great Northern Joint Railway at its own works at Melton Constable in 1904, 1909 and 1910; they were incidentally the last new engines that railway ever had. They had 6ft 0in driving wheels and 17¼ × 24in cylinders. They became LNER 09, 020, and 041, and all were withdrawn in 1942–4.

247 Reid's 4-4-2Ts for the North British Railway, 51 engines of two classes, were built between 1911 and 1921. They had 5ft 9in driving wheels and 18 × 26in cylinders (19in in the later ones). They became BR 67452–67502, and the last survivors were scrapped in 1961.

248 The 4-4-2T was the principal type to be employed on the Belfast & County Down Railway in Ireland; out of its small stock of 30 engines, 15 were of this arrangement. No 9, photographed at Belfast in 1948, was built in 1944, and was by many years the last new 4-4-2T in the British Isles. In the rear of the photograph can be seen No 30, one of the smaller ones, which is now to be seen in Belfast museum.

248

249

4-4-4T

249 The 4-4-4T was a very rarely used type in the British Isles, lack of adhesion being the main trouble, with only about a third of the total engine weight on the coupled wheels. This is best illustrated by the fact that the only railway to build this type to any extent, the North Eastern, eventually found it desirable to rebuild them as 4-6-2Ts. There were 45 of these engines, built between 1913 and 1922. They had 5ft 9in driving wheels

and three 16½ × 26in cylinders, three-cylinder propulsion being most favoured by the designer Sir Vincent Raven. All were converted to 4-6-2Ts between 1931 and 1936. In this form as BR 69850–69894 they lasted until well into the 1950s, a few until 1960.

250 The Metropolitan apparently found the 4-4-4T adequate for its country services into 'Metroland' after the changeover from electric haulage at Harrow (later Rickmansworth) to Aylesbury and Verney Junction. Eight engines were built in 1920 by Kerr Stuart & Co. They had two 19 × 26in outside cylinders and 5ft 9in driving wheels. The Metropolitan became part of London Transport in 1933; the 'main line' engines were taken over by the LNER in 1937, who replaced the 4-4-4Ts with GCR 4-6-2Ts in 1941. They spent their later years in the Nottingham area, the last ones being scrapped in 1947.

250

251 Two 4-4-4Ts were built for the Midland & South Western Junction Railway in 1897, Nos 17 and 18. They became GWR 25 and 27 at the grouping, and were scrapped in 1927 and 1929 respectively.

251

252

of 325 tons on the level, and 110 tons over the hilly section between Donegal and Killybegs. No 10 *Sir James* was photographed at Donegal in 1930. The second engine was No 11 *Hercules*.

253

252 The Wirral Railway had three 4-4-4Ts: No 11, built in 1896 and scrapped in 1919, and a further couple which came out in 1903, Nos 14 and 15. Allocated LMS Nos 6850 and 6851 at the grouping, which they never carried, the latter were withdrawn from service in 1929.

253 A pair of 4-4-4Ts were built for the 3ft 0in gauge of the County Donegal Railway in Ireland in 1902 by Neilsons and worked until 1933. They had 4ft 0in driving wheels, and 14 × 20in cylinders. They could haul trains

0-6-0

From about the 1860s onwards the minimum practicable number of wheels for a locomotive was accepted as six for a tender engine, and the same in general for its tank counterpart. Small four-wheeled tank engines continued however to be used for shunting purposes throughout the history of the steam locomotive. Tender engines for passenger work at that time could be built with a single pair of driving wheels or with four coupled wheels in the 2-4-0 or 0-4-2 configuration. In contrast goods engines normally had all six wheels coupled and this, the 0-6-0, was to become the most widely used type on the whole railway system. By 1913, for instance, there were over 7000 0-6-0 tender engines in service, which with another 3400 of the tank variety, formed 46 per cent of the engine stock in Great Britain. By 1922, just prior to the grouping, this had been reduced to 43 per cent; and in 1947 before nationalisation, to some 4400, about 37 per cent. At this time the 0-6-0 was still the most numerous of any type of wheel arrangement, followed by the 0-6-0T with just over 3000 examples (excluding industrial engines). As a matter of incidental interest the 4-6-0 came third, at that time totalling about 2500. These figures do not include the Irish railways.

In these circumstances it is obviously not practicable within a very limited space to make reference to any but a small proportion of this most widely used of designs, even if this were necessary, as the majority of them had a great deal in common. Attention is focussed on the designs built in the greatest numbers, together with a few examples of unusual or unconventional interest, but some of the major railways must inevitably receive no mention in this section.

The 0-6-0 tender engine was to be found in varying numbers on every railway of major or minor importance apart from the very smallest concerns, which had no tender engines at all, and one notable exception, the Great North of Scotland, which never owned an engine of this type.

254 A suitable start can be made with the Ramsbottom DX goods of the LNWR, which first appeared in 1858. It was constructed in such large numbers that by 1872 no less than 857 had been built at Crewe for the LNWR alone, not to mention another 86 for the L&YR, a rare example of one railway supplying engines for another. This was certainly the earliest example of standardisation of production of a single design. This total of 943 identical engines of one type in fact constitutes a record

254

255

which was never surpassed in Great Britain even in more recent times. Of light and simple construction, they put in many years of hard work, and no less than 88 of them survived the grouping to be allocated LMS Nos 8000–8087; one of them, No 8084, ran until 1930. In addition to these Webb built 500 0-6-0s for purely goods work, with 4ft 5½in wheels and without vacuum brakes; and another 310 mixed traffic engines with 5ft 1½in wheels, often used on passenger trains and usually known as the

'Cauliflowers' owing to the likeness to this vegetable of the LNWR crest which was carried on the centre splasher of the engine (**255**). Examples of both of these classes lasted beyond nationalisation into the mid 1950s.

If ever one individual railway could be said to be dedicated to a particular type of wheel arrangement, the Midland was undoubtedly a 0-6-0 line. For general freight work, from the Kirtley period to the end of its independent existence in 1922 the MR had no other type of goods engine, apart from the imported USA 2-6-0s (see **358**) and indeed the LMS continued to build 0-6-0s of Derby design until 1940. At the time of the 1923 grouping, out of a total of 3019 locomotives, no less than 1570 were 0-6-0 tender engines.

256 The first of Kirtley's double-framed 0-6-0s came out in the 1850s, but what may be regarded as his standard design appeared in 1863. Several hundred were built between that year and 1874. They had 5ft 8in driving wheels, and 16½ × 24in cylinders. All were

257

256

long-lived engines. Those surviving at the 1907 renumbering scheme, including some of his original examples, became Nos 2300–2867, most of them to give many more years of useful service. One or two in fact lasted into nationalisation days, and one survived until 1951 as BR 58110 at the ripe old age of 81. The photograph shows No 478, built in 1862. It later became No 2385 and was scrapped in 1919.

Nos 2707 to 2788 were lent to the Railway Operating Department for overseas service during the First World War, and all returned safely. The engines were reboilered several times during the course of their careers, some with Belpaire fireboxes, as shown by the photograph of No 2852, undoubtedly among the oldest engines to be so fitted (**257**). (In Ireland the GS&WR 0-6-0s, shortly to be described, came within a similar category.)

258 Johnson succeeded Kirtley on the Midland in 1875, and very soon produced his own 0-6-0, with inside frames. This was the basic design which was to become with successive enlargements by far the largest block of engines in Britain, numbered successively 2900–4606, a final total of 1707. Johnson's own engines multiplied over the years, and by 1902 there were 865 of them, not including another 25 for the associated S&DJR and 16 for the M&GNJR. These all carried power classification 2. Many of the Johnson class 2s later received larger boilers, converting them to class 3, with or without Belpaire fireboxes (**259**). Others aquired smaller class 2 boilers with Belpaires (**260**). There was a good deal of interchange between the two classifications, too involved to go into in detail.

260

258

261

259

An enlarged class 3 version appeared in 1903 at the end of Johnson's term of office, and these were continued by his successor Deeley, 70 in all being built between 1903 and 1908. Eventually Fowler brought out the final superheated version in 1911, later generally known as the class 4 goods, although they did a great deal of passenger work as well (**261**). Construction of these continued well into the LMS period until 1940; a total of 772 engines were built, including five for the S&DJR, all virtually identical, a total rarely exceeded in Great Britain.

The history of this remarkable series of engines can best be summarised as follows:

	Built	Numbers from 1907 onwards
Johnson class 2 engines with 4ft 11in driving wheels	1875–87	2900–3019, 3130–3189
Johnson class 2 engines with 5ft 3in driving wheels	1877–1902	3020–3129, 3190–3764
Johnson and Deeley class 3 engines with 5ft 3in driving wheels	1903–8	3765–3834
Fowler engines with 5ft 3in driving wheels	1911–22 1924–40	3835–4026 (MR) 4027–4606 (LMS)

It will be noted that some of the earliest Johnson engines had 4ft 11in wheels. Otherwise the dimensions were standard with 5ft 3in wheels, 18 × 26in cylinders for the Johnsons and 18½ × 26in for the Deeley engines, increased to 20 × 26in in the Fowlers. Boiler pressure was 175lb except for the earlier Johnsons, which had 160lb. One dimension which remained constant throughout was the 16ft 6in wheelbase.

Although some of the Johnson engines remained in service well into the preservation era of the 1960s none of such a deserving historical class was preserved. Three of the Fowlers have survived: the first LMS-built one, No 4027, part of the NRM collection on loan to the Midland Railway centre at Butterley; 3924 on the Keighley & Worth Valley; and 4422 with the North Staffordshire Railway Society.

262   Another railway with a long history of one design of 0-6-0, albeit on a much smaller scale, was the Great Southern and Western. It was the only class of engine on any Irish railway to be built in sufficient numbers to be regarded as a standard type. Designed by A. McDonnell, the first ones appeared in 1866–7. They were built in small numbers over a long period under each of his three successors right up to 1903, by which time there were 111 of them, far more than of any other single design on Irish railways.

These engines bore a striking resemblance to the DXs of the LNWR (see **254**). They had 5ft 2in driving wheels, 18 × 24in cylinders, and 160lb pressure; average dimensions, to be found on almost any 0-6-0 of the latter half of the nineteenth century and the Edwardian period.

Although withdrawals started in 1922, many were modernised in the 1920s and 1930s by the provision of larger Belpaire fireboxes and superheaters, which improved their performance but still allowed them to work on the lightest-laid track. They were probably the oldest engines anywhere to be given such treatment, and were to be found in the 1950s handling branches and excursions as well as general goods work. Their availability ensured that they were among the last steam engines to

262

263

be withdrawn by CIE in 1963. Two have been preserved, No 184, in unrebuilt condition, and No 186, super-heated, the property of the Railway Preservation Society of Ireland; this grand old veteran, now 100 years old, still performs valiant feats in working enthusiasts' steam specials over hundreds of miles of what remains of the Irish railway system, both in the Republic and Northern Ireland (**263**).

264

264 In its early years the Stockton & Darlington Railway favoured what came to be known as the 'long boiler' 0-6-0 of Bouch's design, which dated back to 1864. The last of these came out in 1875. Most of them had 5ft 0in driving wheels and 17 × 26in cylinders after being rebuilt by Worsdell. The final survivor, No 1275, was withdrawn in February 1923 and can be seen in the North Road station museum at Darlington.

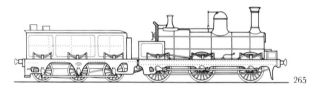

265

265 An interesting experiment at this period was made by Sturrock on the GNR, who provided auxiliary power on some of his 0-6-0s by coupling the six wheels of the tender by outside cranks driven by two additional 12 × 17in inside cylinders. Steam was supplied from the boiler through a pipe to the tender via a second regulator. Several were built in this form between 1863 and 1866, but the idea was not a success owing to the inability of the boiler to provide sufficient steam for two power units. His successor Patrick Stirling quickly removed that serving the tender, converting them to orthodox 0-6-0 engines.

266

267

268

266 Just at the time when the last of the North Eastern long boiler 0-6-0s appeared in 1875, Connor introduced the type on the Caledonian. 39 engines were delivered from the works of Dübs & Co. between 1874 and 1877. They had 5ft 2in wheels and a short wheelbase of only 11 feet; they were broken up between 1898 and 1909.

They were almost unique in British 0-6-0 tender engine design in having outside cylinders. Only one more example was to appear, many years later, and this was a rebuild of an 0-6-0T on the North Staffordshire Railway (see **285**). There were also some outside-cylinder 0-6-0Ts on the Eastern & Midlands Railway, which ran with additional tenders during the 1880s (see **311**).

As with the 4-4-0 type, the Drummond brothers produced a range of broadly similar 0-6-0s for the various railways on which they held the post of locomotive superintendent.

267 Dugald Drummond built 133 0-6-0s for the North British during his term of office on that railway from 1876 to 1883, when he went to the Caledonian, and produced 244 very similar engines up to 1890. These became LMS 17230–17473 at the grouping, and most of them survived into BR days, many of them lasting until the early 1960s. The dome safety valves seen in the photograph of No 17311, taken in 1928, were largely replaced by Ramsbottom valves on the firebox in later days.

He built another 30 almost identical engines for the LSWR in 1897; these were all later rebuilt with large superheated boilers by Urie, as shown in the photograph of S316, temporary number, later 30316, in the first BR style of painting (**268**).

109

269

former, No 673 *Maude* is preserved at Falkirk. No 646 *Somme* was another of a number which served in France during the 1914–18 war, and which were given appropriate commemorative names on their return.

270

271

Peter Drummond produced a series of engines showing a remarkable family likeness for the Highland between 1900 and 1907. They became LMS 17693–17704, the last of which was scrapped in 1951 as BR 57698 (**269**).

The dimensions of all of the above were almost the same, with 5ft 0in wheels, 18 or 18½ × 26in cylinders and working pressure of 175lb or 180lb.

270   Surprisingly the Highland had no other 0-6-0s, but on the Caledonian McIntosh built 96 somewhat larger and very elegant engines between 1899 and 1909, one of which is preserved in Glasgow museum. Pickersgill built 43 with slightly increased dimensions.

271   On the North British Holmes and Reid built many 0-6-0s in the years up to the grouping and one of the

272   On the Great Western a variety of standard gauge 0-6-0s with outside frames were built by Armstrong between 1866 and 1876. Many of these lasted into the 1920s.

272

William Dean designed his own version of the type. Between 1883 and 1899 280 engines were built, Nos 2301–2580, of which all but Nos 2361–2380 had inside frames (**273**).

Generally, these engines had 5ft 0in coupled wheels and 17 × 24in cylinders. Nearly all of them were eventually superheated. 62 engines were loaned to the government for war service overseas in 1917, of which eight never came back, but most lasted into the 1930s and several into the nationalisation period. The last survivor was No 2516, withdrawn in 1956 and now preserved in Swindon museum. Many of these engines were requisitioned for a second spell of wartime duties overseas during the Second World War.

273

274 The GWR built no more 0-6-0s until 1930, when Collett produced a design with the usual GWR coned boiler. 120 were built up till 1948 – the last of the type to be built – and No 3205 is preserved in working order on the Severn Valley Railway.

274

275

275 On the Great Northern both Stirling and Ivatt built a large number of 0-6-0s, of very much the same pattern. The main difference lay in Ivatt's domed boiler, which he fitted to most of Stirling's engines in place of the original domeless pattern. This was the case with No 150A, photographed in 1921 at Strawberry Hill whilst on loan to the London & South Western Railway, and which then still retained the somewhat austere design of cab used by Stirling on his Great Northern Railway engines. There were, with some variations, over 300 of these classes built by both locomotive superintendents between 1871 and 1901.

276 The last class of Great Northern 0-6-0 was Gresley's J6 class, of which 110 were built between 1911 and 1922. With their 5ft 2in wheels, they were much used on passenger trains and general mixed traffic duties.

277 Craven had introduced the 0-6-0 type to the LB&SCR in 1854, followed by Stroudley with his own

278

276

277

design in 1871. R. J. Billinton, who succeeded him in 1890, ordered 20 of a new type to be built by outside firms, of which the Vulcan Foundry won the contract, and these engines appeared in 1893–4 as Nos 433–452. Another 35 came from the same source in 1900 and 1902, Nos 521–555, and the class was always generally known as the Vulcans. They had 5ft 0in wheels and 18×26in cylinders. Most of them were rebuilt by Marsh from 1910 onwards with much larger boilers, transforming them into heavy goods engines (although also often used on passenger duties) comparable to those found on many other railways of this period. Many of them lasted into the early 1960s. Some were fitted with top feed apparatus housed in a second dome (**278**).

279 On the Great Central, 174 0-6-0s were built to Robinson's design between 1901 and 1910. For some obscure reason they were usually known as the Pom-Poms. They had 5ft 2in wheels and $18\frac{1}{2} \times 26$in cylinders. All were eventually superheated, and the whole class survived nationalisation to become 64280–64453, the last being scrapped in 1962. Like many other Robinson engines, they were later much disfigured by the

279

substitution of 'flower pot' type chimneys for the handsome taper design of Great Central days.

280 On the Lancashire & Yorkshire Railway Barton-Wright introduced his standard 0-6-0 in 1876, of which a total of 280 were built between 1876 and 1887. They had 4ft 6in wheels, 17½ × 26in cylinders and 140lb pressure.

When Aspinall became CME at Horwich he produced his own design of 0-6-0, also built in considerable

numbers, but as there was an acute shortage of shunting engines at the time, he rebuilt most of his predecessor's 0-6-0s as saddle tanks (see **306**), although the last 50 of them remained as tender engines. All of them, both rebuilt and unrebuilt, passed into LMS hands in 1923, the saddle tanks becoming 11303–11532, and the tender engines 12025–12064. Many of both varieties survived into nationalisation.

The last 0-6-0, BR No 52044, originally L&YR 957 was not withdrawn until 1959. It was acquired for preservation and can now be seen on the Keighley & Worth Valley Railway, who also have one of the rebuilt saddle tanks. One of the later Aspinall 0-6-0s has also survived and is currently housed at Steamtown, Carnforth (**281**).

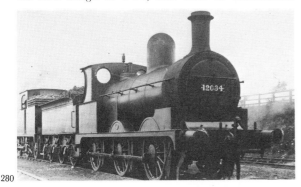

280

281

282 Of the 201 class J21 0-6-0s of the North Eastern Railway, built by T. W. Worsdell between 1886 and 1895, all but 30 were originally two-cylinder Von Borries compounds, but had been rebuilt as simples by 1913. In this form many of them were modernised with the provision of superheaters, and in some cases piston valves. In later years the cylinders varied between 18 × 24in and 19 × 26½in. The driving wheels were 5ft 1in.

The survivors were allocated BR Nos 65025–65123. No 65098 was photographed at Tebay in 1951 on arrival from Darlington over Stainmore summit, a hilly line (now closed) over which these engines were predominant for many years. The last survivor, 65033, withdrawn in 1962, is preserved in working order at Beamish Museum, Durham, restored as NER 876.

283 Later North Eastern 0-6-0s included 165 of classes J26 and J27, powerful engines with small wheels for heavy mineral traffic. Several of the latter lasted almost to the end of steam on BR and one is to be seen on the North Yorkshire Moors Railway, restored as NER 2392.

284 A very typical design of 0-6-0 of the middle Edwardian period was the SE&CR C class, Wainwright's first new engines after he became locomotive superintendent following the joint working agreement between the SER and the LC&DR. A good, straightforward and very handsome design capable of hard work over the none-too-easy lines of the system, these engines could at times be seen on express passenger work. They had 5ft 2in driving wheels, 18½ × 26in cylinders and 160lb pressure.

No 486 was photographed in 1926, still in wartime grey livery. They underwent little change, except for one engine which was converted to a saddle tank. The last survivors went in the 1960s, but No 592 is preserved in working order on the Bluebell Railway.

282

283

284

285

286

287

285 There was a complete absence of any new British design of 0-6-0 tender engine with outside cylinders after the 1870s. One four-cylinder engine was however made by the rebuilding of a tank locomotive. Further details of this solitary North Staffordshire engine will be given in the section dealing with 0-6-0Ts in general (see **320**). No 2367, as it became in the LMS list on rebuilding as a tender engine in 1924, was renumbered 8689 in 1928 but scrapped in the same year after a total life of only six years.

286 The Great Eastern Y14 (later LNER J15) class 0-6-0 was designed by T. W. Worsdell. The type was continued by his successors, J. Holden and S. D. Holden, until there were 289 of them, built between 1883 and 1913. They had 4ft 11in driving wheels and 17½ × 24in cylinders. They changed little over the years except for the substitution of lipped chimneys for the earlier stovepipe pattern, and of Ross safety valves for the Ramsbottom type. Some acquired side window cabs to give better protection on the footplate. 43 of them were loaned to the government during the First World War. 272 were still in service at the 1923 grouping and 130 at nationalisation to be allocated BR Nos 65350–65479.

During their long careers they formed an essential part of the railway scene in East Anglia, and could be seen on all kinds of duties, essentially maids-of-all-work. Their somewhat diminutive and elderly appearance belied the feats of haulage of which they were capable. No 887 was photographed in the temporary wartime grey livery. Of the last four survivors in 1962, No 65462 was obtained for preservation by the North Norfolk Railway at Sheringham, now restored as GER 564.

287 The most powerful pregrouping 0-6-0s to be built were 25 engines on the Great Eastern Railway designed by A. J. Hill, Nos 1270–1294, which came out between 1920 and 1922. These had 4ft 11in wheels, and 20 × 28in cylinders; their maximum tractive effort of 29045lb was to be exceeded only by Bulleid's Q1s on the Southern in 1942. No 1287 was photographed as LNER 8287 in 1937. Gresley substituted round-topped fireboxes from 1943 onwards. The class became BR 64675–64699 and were withdrawn between 1959 and 1962.

288

288 Gresley's standard mixed traffic 0-6-0 was the class J39, which had 5ft 2in wheels, 20 × 26in cylinders and 180lb pressure. 289 engines were built between 1921 and 1937. They became BR 64700–64988, the last survivors being scrapped in the early 1960s.

There was also a 4ft 8in version, the J38, for heavy mineral work on the Fife lines of the North British; these had a 6in longer boiler, the smokebox being shortened by the same amount. The tractive effort of these engines was not far short of the GER class J20s already mentioned. As BR 65900–65934 some of them lasted until the end of steam in Scotland in 1967.

289 The last design of 0-6-0 to appear in the British Isles were Bulleid's Austerities of 1942, with the unenviable reputation of being perhaps the ugliest engine ever to be seen in Britain. No 33025 was photographed in 1948 at Eastleigh. Nevertheless, despite their unprepossessing appearance they were extremely efficient machines and fully met the requirements for which they were built under wartime conditions.

They were powerful general purpose engines with a high route availability. A maximum weight of 51 tons in working order was achieved by elimination of running plates and any other features which could be dispensed with. They had 5ft 1in wheels, which, with 19 × 26in cylinders, produced a tractive effort of 30080lb; the highest ever achieved by a British 0-6-0. Built as Nos C1–C40, they received conventional numbers 33001–33040 after nationalisation, and all lasted until 1963–6. The original C1 has been preserved as part of

289

the NRM collection, at present on loan to the Bluebell Railway.

0-6-0T

The 0-6-0T was the most widely used type of any in the British Isles. It was to be found in varying numbers on every public railway, major or minor, not to mention the several thousand built over the years for industrial concerns, for collieries, steelworks and the like.

So far as the main line railways are concerned, the Great Western was the largest user and from the close of the century right through the period of the heyday of steam they maintained a stock of around a thousand at any one time until they began to be displaced by the inevitable diesels. They were to be found all over the system engaged on all manner of duties, both passenger and goods.

In all, some 2400 were constructed between the years 1860 and 1956. They comprised a wide range of varieties, mostly saddle tanks or the more modern square-shaped pannier tanks, although there were also a certain number of side tanks. The earlier engines were mostly double framed, whereas the later were single framed. Some were even built for the broad gauge, convertible to standard gauge when the need arose. The variety was endless, and a fuller description of the types would necessitate a full volume in itself; one has in fact been published.

290 Typical of William Dean's designs with double frames, No 1670 was built in 1886 with 5ft 0in wheels and 17 × 26in cylinders. Similar engines had 4ft 1½in and 4ft 7½in wheels, and these dimensions are representative of the whole range of these engines. The majority of

the saddle tanks survived to be converted to pannier tanks, and a number were superheated; this particular one happens to have been scrapped in 1911 without being so treated.

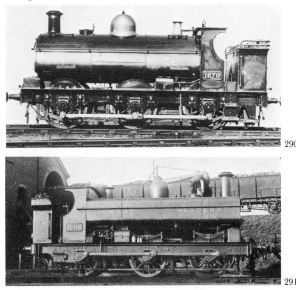

290

291

291 No 1026 was a much earlier engine of 1867, converted to a pannier tank in 1919 and scrapped in 1931.

292 No 2007 was a single-framed example built in 1892. It retained its saddle tank until it was broken up in

117

292

1949, one of the few of its particular class never to be rebuilt with pannier tanks.

293 The last of what may be termed the earlier generation of saddle tanks was built in 1905, but after a lapse of 24 years construction was resumed with a standard design, the 5700 class. Basically the same as the earlier single-framed engines, they had 4ft 7½in wheels, 17½ × 24in cylinders, and 200lb pressure. Several hundreds of them were built up to 1950. No 9608, photographed in 1957, typifies the class. There were also others with some variations; some were fitted with 5ft 2in wheels for passenger work on push-pull trains, and others had 4ft 1½in wheels for increased power.

Between 1956 and 1963, 13 of the 5700 class were sold to London Transport, and some of these remained in service until 1971, several years after the last of them had disappeared from British Railways itself. A few of them were acquired by preservation societies on their ultimate withdrawal and can be seen in active service at various locations around the country.

293

294

294 A final updated version appeared in 1947 with the Swindon domeless taper boiler. The 9400 class comprised 210 engines, Nos 9400–9499, 8400–8499, and 3400–3409; their main dimensions were the same as the 5700 class. No 3409, which came out as late as 1956, was the last engine of pure Great Western design ever to be built. Their late appearance on the scene after dieselisation was already under way led to their having very short lives. No 9400 is preserved in Swindon museum, and No 9466 at Quainton Road.

295 Even this was not quite the end of the GWR pannier tank story, as Hawksworth had turned out ten engines in 1949, Nos 1500–1509. These differed from their predecessors in several respects, notably in the use of outside cylinders, seen before on only a very few specimens of the type on the GWR. Other innovations included the use of Walschaert's valve gear and the absence of a running plate. They had 4ft 7½in wheels, 17½ × 24in cylinders and 200lb pressure. No 1501 survives on the Severn Valley Railway.

296 The GWR's stock of 0-6-0 tank engines was further augmented at the grouping by the acquisition of some 150 examples from the South Wales railways. These engines were a somewhat miscellaneous collection.

Of particular interest were three from the Taff Vale, built in 1884 for the Pwllyrhebog incline, 1¾ miles long with gradients of between 1 in 13 and 1 in 30. This was worked on a counterbalancing principle with a cable passing round a drum at the summit connected to an ascending and descending train, each with one of these locomotives attached, the one going down providing brake power. These engines were notable in being the first to be fitted with coned boilers. They had 5ft 3in driving wheels and 17½ × 26in cylinders. No 143, later GWR 792 and finally 193, was sold to the National Coal Board on withdrawal in 1951, when the incline closed, and was not cut up until 1960.

297 The standard shunting engines on the LNWR during the earlier Webb regime were the Special Tanks,

295

296

297

actually designed by Ramsbottom and built from 1870 onwards, of which 258 had appeared by 1880. They had 4ft 3in wheels and 17 × 24in cylinders. About 265 remained at the grouping to be allocated LMS Nos 7220–7457, together with a few others attached to the Departmental Stock for use at Wolverton and other carriage works. Some of these remained in service until 1959, but the last of the main series had gone by 1941. Right up to the 1920s they were to be seen on empty carriage working at Euston.

No 3234, built in 1874 as No 2130, was photographed in original condition without cab. Allotted LMS No 7322, it never carried the number as it was scrapped in 1925.

298 Six somewhat similar engines were supplied to the Dundalk Newry & Greenore Railway in Ireland, which

298

was owned by the LNWR, between 1873 and 1898. Although of obvious Crewe design they were not exactly like any to be found on the parent system, being best described as a cross between a DX goods (see **254**) and the Special Tanks just described. They had 5ft 2½in wheels and 17 × 22in cylinders. Of the six built between 1873 and 1898, all but one lasted until 1952. No 4 *Newry* was photographed at Newry in 1952. All retained their LNWR livery and characteristics to the end.

299 The Midland was another large user of 0-6-0Ts, although on nothing like the scale of the GWR.

A very ancient survivor in later years was No 1601, a Kirtley engine built as long ago as 1848 by E. S. Wilson & Co. which, along with one or two others lasted after several rebuildings into early LMS days. It was by far the oldest engine still at work at the amalgamation. It had 4ft 2in driving wheels and 15 × 22in cylinders.

300 Johnson's standard design of 0-6-0T was introduced in 1874. Progressively enlarged, they continued to be built up to 1902, by which time they totalled 340, Nos 1620–1959. They had 4ft 7in driving wheels, 17 × 24in cylinders and pressure from 140lb to 160lb. Many of these engines, especially the later ones, received Belpaire fireboxes and pop safety valves in place of Johnson's design with Salter valves mounted on the dome. No 1708, built in 1880, is preserved by the 1708 Preservation Trust, at the premises of the Midland Railway Trust, Butterley, Derby.

Some of the London based engines were fitted with condensing apparatus for working through the Metropolitan line tunnels (**301**).

Although withdrawals started in 1920, there were still

155 in service in 1948, and the last ones survived until 1966, at which time they were the oldest of British Railways' rapidly dwindling steam stock.

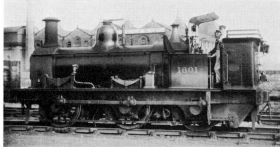

299

300

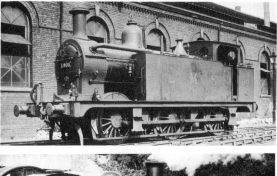

301

302

302 A slightly modified version of the last of Johnson's 0-6-0Ts, but with the same principal dimensions, the chief difference being the extended smokebox, was adopted by the LMS after the grouping as a standard shunting design. 415 of them were built between 1924 and 1931, Nos 7100–7149, 16400–16764, plus another seven for the S&DJR, Nos 19–25. All of these were eventually incorporated into one series as BR 47260–47681.

A few went overseas during the Second World War, of which three never came back, and two were sold to the NCC in Northern Ireland in 1944, suitably regauged to 5ft 3in, but nearly all the others lasted until the 1960s. Some of these are now to be found at various preservation centres, including three with the Midland Railway Trust at Butterley. One of these latter engines has been attractively repainted in Midland red with its original number 16440, although the class were always in black livery in actual service.

303 William Stroudley is best known as locomotive superintendent of the LB&SCR from 1870–89, but he had previously spent two or three years on the Highland, on which line he produced his first design, a small 0-6-0T which was the forerunner of his famous Terriers built when he went to Brighton.

303

The first of his Highland Railway engines emerged from Lochgorm works in 1869, No 56 *Balnain*, followed by two more after his departure, No 57 *Lochgorm* and 49 *Fort George* in 1872 and 1874. They had 3ft 8in driving wheels and 14 × 20in cylinders, with 120lb pressure. All survived the grouping, and *Lochgorm* was photographed as LMS 16119 in 1930. It ran until 1932.

304 The Brighton Terriers hardly need any introduction. The first of them came out in 1872 and by 1880 there were 50 of them, Nos 35–84. No 41 *Piccadilly* is shown in its original condition. They were built originally for work in the London suburban area, which they performed for many years, although their later uses were more varied. Many were sold out of service to various light railways and industrial organisations; their history is too complicated to go into detail here. A number were retained for branch line and miscellaneous duties, and these underwent little alteration except that most of the later survivors received extended smokeboxes and a number were fitted with push-pull apparatus for motor train working. Their basic dimensions were 4ft 0in driving wheels, 12 × 20in cylinders (later increased to 13 × 20in or 14 × 20in on some engines) and 150lb pressure.

After the grouping several were transferred to the Isle of Wight. At nationalisation about a dozen still remained to come into BR stock; several of these were in traffic until 1963, mainly working the Hayling Island branch, their last regular job, which closed in that year.

No 80 *Boxhill*, restored to original condition, can be seen in York museum, but the type was so suitable for operation on light preserved railways that the last survivors were eagerly sought after by preservation societies. As a result, no less than ten of the original 50 are still in

304

305

306

existence, mostly in working order, principally on the Bluebell and Kent & East Sussex Railways. No 54 *Waddon* is in Canada, and No 46 *Newington* stands outside a hostelry on Hayling Island; known as the *Hayling Billy* it is a remarkable and unique public house sign.

Stroudley's Terriers were followed by a much enlarged version for general use, the E1 class consisting of 78 engines built between 1874 and 1891. One of them has survived and can be seen on the East Somerset Railway.

305 L. B. Billinton produced ten much more modern 0-6-0Ts for the LB&SCR between 1913 and 1916, the class E2, Nos 100–109. These had 4ft 6in wheels and 17½ × 26in cylinders, with 170lb pressure; all were at work until the early 1960s.

306 Barton Wright's numerous 0-6-0s for the L&YR have already been described (see **280**), along with the fact that the majority of them were converted by Aspinall to saddle tanks. No 11324 was photographed in 1953; it was at that time one of the Horwich works engines.

307 The first six-coupled tanks on the LSWR appeared in 1876 to the design of W. G. Beattie. These were saddle tanks, with 4ft 1in wheels and 17 × 24in cylinders. There were 20 of them, built up to 1882, all from the works of Messrs Beyer Peacock. They were long-lived engines; amongst other duties they shunted continually in Nine Elms yard right through to the 1920s. Five of them were rebuilt by Drummond with his individual style of pop safety valves mounted on the dome, and his own chimney replacing the stove pipe fitted by Adams. No 0333, photographed at Eastleigh in 1927, was so rebuilt.

The last of these engines to remain in service was No 0335, as Kent & East Sussex No 4, to which railway it had been exchanged for a 0-8-0T in 1932 (see **511**). It was still in serviceable condition if not actually at work in 1948, when the K&ESR was absorbed by BR (**308**).

309 On the GNR both Stirling and Ivatt adopted the 0-6-0ST as the standard shunting engine, and between them built 264 from 1868 to 1909. They were all of much the same general design but with some variations and of progressively increased dimensions.

The Stirling engines were all domeless in accordance with tradition, whereas Ivatt provided his with domes and rebuilt many of his predecessor's machines in like fashion. No 3155A, a later Stirling engine of 1897, was rebuilt so as to be almost indistinguishable from the Ivatt version.

The survivors in 1948 were allocated BR Nos 68757–68889, but very few lasted beyond the 1950s. No 1247, an Ivatt-built loco, has been preserved and can be seen on the North Yorkshire Moors Railway.

307

308

309

124

310

311

312

310 Gresley added to the fleet of Great Northern shunting engines by the construction of 102 0-6-0Ts between 1913 and 1930, generally known as the Ardsley Tanks. They had 4ft 8in wheels, $18\frac{1}{2} \times 26$in cylinders, and 175lb pressure. As BR 68890–68991 the majority of them lasted into the early 1960s.

311 In 1873 18 0-6-0Ts were supplied by Messrs Sharp Stewart & Co. to the Cornwall Minerals Railway. Designed to work in pairs, back to back, they had 3ft 6in driving wheels and $16\frac{1}{4} \times 20$in cylinders. When the Great Western took over the Cornwall Minerals in 1877 it kept nine of them and rebuilt them as saddle tanks to become GWR 1392–1400, most of which remained in service until the 1930s.

The other nine were returned to the makers, who disposed of them to the Lynn & Fakenham Railway, together with additional tenders, making them temporarily outside-cylinder 0-6-0 tender engines, a rarity in British practice. One of them was photographed running in this form as Eastern & Midlands No 12A. They were later rebuilt as 2-4-0s with the side tanks removed, and

although taken out of service between 1898 and 1905 parts of them were used in the construction of new 0-6-0Ts. These were nominally regarded as rebuilds, the works plates actually bearing the inscription 'Rebuilt Melton Constable' and the appropriate date. No 15 was photographed in 1937 (**312**). In this form they survived to be taken into LNER stock and were scrapped during the 1940s.

313

314

315

313 The SE&CR on its formation in 1900 inherited ten 0-6-0Ts from the LC&DR which had been built by Kirtley in 1879, Nos 141–150, which became 600–609 under the new regime. These had 4ft 6in wheels and 17 × 24in cylinders. All survived into Southern Railway days; when being taken out of service in 1951, No 1600 was sold to the National Coal Board and worked at Haydock Colliery in Lancashire until 1958.

314 James Stirling built 25 0-6-0Ts for the South Eastern Railway between 1888 and 1898. They had 5ft 2in wheels and 18 × 26in cylinders. Most of them later received domed boilers, but No 1155, photographed in 1934, still retained the typical Stirling domeless pattern. They were scrapped at various dates between 1914 and 1960.

315 Wainwright's only 0-6-0Ts for the SE&CR consisted of eight small engines for light branch line use, built in 1905–6. They could possibly be regarded as a modernised version of the LB&SCR Terriers (see **304**). They had 3ft 9in wheels and 12 × 18in cylinders. No less than four of them have survived for preservation, two on the Bluebell Railway and two on the Kent & East Sussex Railway. No 31323, photographed at Ashford in 1952, is now running on the Bluebell line.

316 Three little-known engines which appeared from Lochgorm works in 1903–4 were of unusual interest with their 5ft 3in driving wheels, somewhat large for shunting duties, resulting from the re-use of parts of scrapped 2-4-0s. This was an economy made necessary by the impecunious state of the company's finances. They had 18 × 24in outside cylinders, and lasted until 1930–2 as LMS 16380–16382.

316

Together with the three Stroudley engines already mentioned these were the only 0-6-0Ts the Highland ever had, an unusually small proportion of the total stock of 173 engines at the grouping.

317 On the Great Eastern James Holden introduced his 0-6-0Ts in 1886. There were ultimately 249 in all, of five classes, LNER J65 to J69, but basically of the same design. They all had 4ft 0in driving wheels, the dimensions in the later series progressively increasing from 14 × 20in cylinders to 16½ × 22in, and working pressure from 160lb to 180lb. The last ten to be built came out under Hill's superintendency in 1914.

In later years there was a certain amount of rebuilding and interchange between the classes. A lot of them spent many years on the busy suburban services out of Liverpool Street, for which purpose they had Westinghouse brakes, as well as goods work and general shunting duties all over the system in East Anglia. In later LNER days several went to Scotland.

About 150 remained to become BR locomotives at nationalisation, and one of them, BR E8619 (later 68619) was specially painted in apple green livery and later in GER royal blue, and kept in spick and span condition for acting as a station pilot until its withdrawal in 1961, one of the last to remain in traffic (**318**). Another example, restored to its original condition as GER 87, can be seen in York museum.

317

318

319

319 A North Eastern design of 0-6-0T introduced by Wilson Worsdell in 1898 stands unique in being constructed over a period of no less than 53 years under three successive stages of railway ownership and five regimes of locomotive management. The first 20 came out in 1898–9, after which no more were built until 1914, by which time Sir Vincent Raven was in charge. Others followed in 1920 and 1922, and after the grouping Gresley built another ten at Doncaster, bringing the total up to 85. These became BR 68670–68754 at nationalisation.

Even more remarkably BR added yet another 28 under the superintendency of Peppercorn, who had succeeded Thompson as temporary CME of the Eastern and North Eastern regions of British Railways. They were built between 1949 and 1951, and received the numbers 69001–69028, as no provision had been made in the numbering scheme to enable them to follow the block of numbers allocated to the original engines. Owing to the onset of dieselisation they inevitably had very short lives of little more than ten years.

All of these engines were practically identical with the original 1898 design without modern improvements or modifications. They had 4ft 1¾in wheels and 18 × 24in cylinders.

The illustration shows No 68680 in fully lined out green livery for station pilot duty at Newcastle. No 69023 has been preserved with the name *Joem* and now works a passenger service on the Derwent Valley Railway, York.

320 In 1922 Mr Hookham of the North Staffordshire Railway built an experimental engine intended for suburban duties around Stoke-on-Trent. It was unique in being the only four-cylinder 0-6-0T ever to appear in the British Isles. It had 4ft 6in driving wheels, four 14 × 24in cylinders and 175lb pressure. The cylinder cranks were set at an angle which produced eight beats per revolution of the driving wheels instead of the usual four (anticipating the SR Lord Nelsons). The engine

320

does not appear to have been a success, and it was rebuilt as a tender engine in 1924 (see **285**).

321 During the Second World War a standard class of 0-6-0ST was evolved for general use at the various war establishments both at home and abroad. The class had 4ft 3in driving wheels and 18 × 26in cylinders, and 170–175lb pressure. No 132 *Sapper* was photographed at Bicester Ordnance Depot. Many hundreds were built from 1943 onwards, and production continued after the war for general industrial use, in particular for the National Coal Board. After the war 75 of them were purchased by the LNER, to become BR Nos 68006–68080.

A slightly more powerful version appeared in 1950 with 4ft 0in driving wheels and pressure increased to 180lb (**322**). The final one to appear was in 1964 for the Cadeby Main Colliery, and is noteworthy in being the last standard gauge steam locomotive ever to be built for use in this country. It can now be seen at Quainton Road.

322

The design proved eminently suitable for preserved lines, with the result that they are to be found all over Britain. Their numbers have grown so much that they now total about 50 in all, by far the most numerous preserved class anywhere, greatly exceeding even the Hunslet 0-4-0STs (see **65**).

At the time of writing there are still a few of them to be found in commercial use at industrial locations, where steam has not yet entirely disappeared.

323 Another design built for war requirements came from the USA, in this case a typically American 0-6-0T with outside cylinders and bar frames. They had 4ft 6in wheels, 16¼ × 24in cylinders, and 210lb pressure. When they became surplus after the war 14 were purchased by the Southern Railway for use at Southampton Docks, to supersede an equivalent number of Adams 0-4-0Ts (see **57**). They were in turn to be eventually replaced by diesels.

321

323

324

325

Two were transferred by BR as departmental list No DS237 *Wainwright* and DS238 *Maunsell* as shunters at Ashford works. Both of these are now on the Kent & East Sussex Railway, and two others have been acquired, SR No 72 by the Keighley & Worth Valley Railway and BR 30064 by the Bluebell Railway. No 4372 was photographed while awaiting disposal at Newbury in 1947.

324 One of the many thousands of industrial 0-6-0T which have appeared in the British Isles, an early 0-6-0ST was built in 1879 by Messrs Beyer Peacock & Co. The engine was photographed at Treeton, Yorks in 1957. This was one of a group of collieries in the district under the management of the Rothervale Collieries, Rotherham, who numbered its engines rather unusually from No 0 to No 9. *Rothervale* No 0 was a long-lived engine, scrapped in 1959, and was one of the few engines built by Beyer Peacock for industrial use.

325 The firm of Manning Wardle & Co., of Leeds, established in 1858, built about 2000 locomotives over the years, nearly all for industrial use. The majority of these were inside-cylinder 0-6-0STs of the same basic design which was gradually enlarged and improved over nearly 70 years. Indeed its development could be said to have continued with Kitson and Hunslet engines of the 1930s, eventually forming the basic Riddles design for the war department, culminating with the last steam engine built for commercial use in this country, in 1964.

The last Manning Wardle engine appeared in 1926 under works No 2047, for the Rugby Portland Cement Company. It was secured for preservation in 1968 and is now to be seen on the Severn Valley Railway named *Warwickshire*, and painted in royal blue livery. Its dimensions were fairly typical of such engines, with 3ft 6in wheels, 14 × 20in cylinders, 160lb pressure, and with a weight of 30 tons.

326 Messrs Robert Stephenson & Hawthorne Ltd was the result of an amalgamation in 1937 of the old-established firm of Hawthorne Leslie & Co. with the original Robert Stephenson & Co., founded as long ago as 1823 at Darlington, virtually the birthplace of the steam locomotive. They continued to supply powerful shunting engines, mainly 0-6-0Ts with outside cylinders, until 1955, typical of which is No 7597 of 1949, now to be seen on the Stour Valley Line at Chappel and Wakes Colne. They had 3ft 8in wheels, 18 × 24in cylinders, 175lb pressure, and weighed 52 tons.

327 Between 1889 and 1906 Messrs Manning Wardle & Co supplied three 0-6-0STs for the 3ft 0in gauge system of the Kettering Iron & Coal Co., which served the nearby ironstone quarries. The works closed in 1963, and the third of these locomotives, No 8, has been preserved by the Kettering Corporation Museum.

0-6-2T

The 0-6-2T, or radial tank, as it was sometimes known, was a type favoured by many railways for local passenger work, and also to some extent for goods and shunting duties.

328 By far the most numerous were to be found on the LNWR, 380 engines in all, the work of F. W. Webb. Whatever the deficiencies of his compound locomotives, when he turned his attention to simple propulsion he was able to produce a sound design which could provide

326

327

328

many years of useful and reliable service. Such was the case with his two classes of 0-6-2T.

The first of them was the 4ft 5½in engine, introduced in 1881, of which no less than 300 were to come out by 1896. Although intended mainly for goods work, they were also frequently used on passenger duties, some even being fitted with push-pull apparatus in later years. Right up to and after nationalisation they were to be found working valiantly alongside much larger 0-8-0s on the hilly line between Abergavenny and Merthyr in South Wales. The last survivor, as BR 58926, which worked a final commemorative special over the route in 1956, has been restored to original condition as LNWR 1054 and is currently to be found at the Dinting Railway Centre.

329 The passenger variety, with 5ft 0in driving wheels, was introduced in 1898 and consisted of 80 engines built up to the year 1902. Like their smaller contemporaries, they remained practically unaltered throughout their existence; a few lasted into BR days, the final survivor being No 46900, photographed at Birmingham New Street in 1951. This engine was scrapped in 1953.

330

329

330 The second largest user of the 0-6-2T was the Taff Vale in South Wales. The type was first introduced in 1885 by Mr Hurry Riches, and thereafter built by him in considerable numbers, of progressive classes, until his death in 1911. The type was continued by his successor, Mr J. Cameron, until the year 1922 and amalgamation with the GWR. By this time, of the total of 271 locomotives owned by the Taff Vale, no less than 209 were 0-6-2Ts.

A representative example is GWR No 302, originally TVR No 104, of class O4 built by Peacock & Co. in 1908, photographed at Treherbert in 1938 and scrapped in 1948. It had 4ft 6½in driving wheels and 17½ × 26in cylinders. Many of them were 'Swindonised' with GWR taper boilers in later years.

331 The GWR had no 0-6-2Ts of its own design prior to the grouping, when it inherited a considerable number from the South Wales valley lines, particularly the Taff Vale, as already recounted. In the cause of standardisation, Collett produced his own version in 1924, of which 200 were eventually built, numbered 5600–5699 and 6600–6699 in accordance with the general pattern of the GWR numbering scheme, the second digit supposed to

331

represent as far as possible a particular class (i.e. if there had been any more of them they would have been numbered 7600 upwards). These engines, with typical Swindon characteristics, had 18 × 26in cylinders and 4ft 7½in driving wheels. They replaced many of the miscellaneous collection acquired from independent lines in South Wales, although they were to be found on the other parts of the system as well. Two or three have survived for preservation, including No 6697, to be found at the Didcot Railway Centre.

332 Mr J. Parker introduced the 0-6-2T to the Manchester Sheffield and Lincolnshire Railway in 1889. A revised version appeared in 1891, of considerable importance in that it was the first engine in the country to be provided with a Belpaire firebox, the purpose of which was to provide increased heating surface. This lead was followed in due course by Aspinall on the L&YR, Dean and Churchward on the GWR, Johnson on the MR, and others. Several locomotive designers however never adopted it, among them Ivatt on the GNR, followed by Gresley and his successors Thompson and Peppercorn

on the LNER; also McIntosh, Pickersgill, Raven, or either of the Drummonds. As a result, no engine of the GNR, CR, GNoSR or NER (except for a pair of compound Atlantics) ever ran with a Belpaire firebox. This was also the case on the North British, apart from the Reid Atlantics, and it did not appear on the LNWR, LBSC, G&SWR or Highland until later years.

332

333

The MS&L 0-6-2Ts eventually totalled 184 engines, including some built in 1900 after it had become the Great Central Railway. There were also another 18 built for the Lancashire Derbyshire & East Coast Railway, absorbed by the Great Central in 1907. All survived the grouping, but the LD&ECR ones all went during the 1930s. Most of the others lasted until the nationalisation era, to become BR 69225–69370, of which a few were in service up to 1960 (**333**). They had 5ft 1in driving wheels and 18 × 26in cylinders.

334 Of the three major railways forming the Southern group the only one to adopt the 0-6-2T was the LBSC, which it did extensively with the type accounting for a total of 134 out of 615 engines at the grouping. They were of four main varieties: two classes, E3 and E6, were designed for goods work with 4ft 6in driving wheels; two were designed for passenger work, the E4 and E5 with 5ft 0in and 5ft 6in driving wheels respectively. A few E5s and E6s subsequently received larger boilers, being reclassified E5x and E6x, and most of the E3s and E4s received extended smokeboxes and some boiler modifications, otherwise remaining largely unaltered.

The first E3 was actually designed by Stroudley in 1891, but all except the original one were built under the regime of R. J. Billinton, the last coming out in 1905. No 158 was photographed at Littlehampton in 1927. All originally had names displayed on the tank sides, but as with most other Brighton engines, Marsh removed them when he assumed charge in 1905. Such were the excellent wearing qualities of the Stroudley yellow livery that one engine 591 *Tillington* of class E5, retained it as late as 1917. This class, with its 5ft 6in driving wheels, of which No 584 *Lordington* is an example (**335**), were fast runners,

and were often used on semi-main line duties. Several ran as 2-4-2Ts for a time by the simple expedient of removing the front coupling rods.

All of the 0-6-2Ts except the original Stroudley engine survived nationalisation, the last one being withdrawn as late as 1963. One of the E4s survives on the Bluebell Railway, restored as LBSC 473 *Birch Grove*.

334

335

336

337

338

336 It should be mentioned that the ranks of 0-6-2Ts of LB&SCR origin were increased in SR days by the rebuilding in 1927–9 of ten of Stroudley's E1 class 0-6-0Ts, dating back to the 1870s and 1880s, with radial trailing wheels for service in the West Country. These were reclassified E1R and worked until the 1950s.

337 0-6-2Ts, like other six-driving-wheel front-coupled engines, almost invariably had inside cylinders, so it is worth illustrating one of the rare exceptions. Two outside-cylinder engines were built for the Plymouth Devonport & South Western Junction Railway in 1907; they had 4ft 0in driving wheels and 16 × 24in cylinders. They survived to become BR Nos 30757 and 30758, and were scrapped in 1957. *Lord St Levan*, as SR 758, was photographed at Plymouth Friary in 1927; the other engine was *Earl of Mount Edgecumbe*.

338 On the GNR Ivatt introduced the 0-6-2T in 1907, mainly for London suburban work; by 1912 there were 55 of them. They had 5ft 8in driving wheels and 18 × 26in cylinders, and those working in the London area had condensing apparatus. In later years a number were allocated to the West Riding of Yorkshire. Known as the N1 class, they became BR 69430–69485 and all lasted into the 1950s.

339 In 1920 Gresley produced a larger version, the N2, of which 60 were built as GNR engines. These were followed in 1925 by another 47, new to the LNER. Most of the earlier ones were allocated to the London area, replacing the 4-4-2Ts which went to country districts, and many of the LNER-built ones were destined for other parts of the system, notably the Great Eastern and

339

340

341

Scotland, for which purpose they were fitted with Westinghouse brakes. The N2s eventually became BR 69490–69596, and were taken out of service between 1955 and 1962. No 69523, restored as LNER 4744, can be seen at work on the Great Central Railway Main Line Trust at Loughborough.

340 In 1914 A. J. Hill, of the Great Eastern, designed an 0-6-2T for the busy suburban services out of Liverpool Street, with the idea of eventually replacing the existing 2-4-2Ts, 0-4-4Ts, and 0-6-0Ts on their onerous duties; the 2-4-2Ts however still appeared on these trains until the onset of electrification in 1947. Only 12 of the 0-6-2Ts were built prior to the grouping, GER Nos 1000–1011, although another ten were under construction, and came out as LNER 990E–999E.

Gresley, the new CME, was a broad-minded man, sufficiently so to recognise the merits of the design, and he built another 112 of them between 1925 and 1928, with certain minor modifications (**341**). The original No 1000 used saturated steam for trials against No 1001 which was fitted with a Robinson superheater, eventually applied to the whole of the class. They had 4ft 10in driving wheels and 18 × 24in cylinders. The later ones had round-topped fireboxes in place of Belpaires, which Gresley seems to have always disliked, and most of the earlier ones were later so converted.

As BR Nos 69600–69733 all were in service until the late 1950s and early 1960s. One of the original engines survives on the Stour Valley Preservation Society line as GER 999.

It is not possible to describe and illustrate many other railways' 0-6-2T engines beyond quoting some figures for the number in existence at the time of the 1923 grouping, after which very few new ones appeared apart from those on the GER and GWR already described.

The NER for instance had 102, the NBR 75, the Barry 72, Rhymney 53, the NSR 34, the G&SWR 29, the H&BR 24, the L&YR 21, the MR 14 (former LT&SR engines) and the Metropolitan four; some of the other South Wales lines and the Irish railways also had them in small numbers.

0-6-4T

342 The 0-6-4T was not a widely used type in the United Kingdom. Deeley built 40 of them for the Midland Railway in 1907, but it must be regarded as one of the few unsuccessful designs ever to appear on that railway. They were of course intended as large suburban

342

tank engines to replace the 0-4-4Ts; this they never succeeded in doing to any extent. They were tried out with varying success in the Manchester, Birmingham and London areas, including the Tilbury section.

Their long side tanks extending the whole length of the boiler and smokebox made them unsteady riders and eventually, after a few derailments, they were restricted to freight traffic. They earned for themselves the nickname of Flat Irons. They were rebuilt by Fowler with superheaters and extended smokeboxes during the 1920s, but the last of them disappeared in 1938.

They had 5ft 7in driving wheels and $18\frac{1}{2} \times 26$in cylinders, and were numbered 2000–2039.

343 Amongst the earliest 0-6-4Ts to appear were those of the Mersey Railway, built in 1885 for the opening of the underground railway linking Liverpool and Birkenhead, which involved negotiating gradients of 1 in 27 with 150-ton trains. In view of the amount of tunnel work they were fitted with condensing apparatus, as with engines working over the Metropolitan lines in London. They were very powerful locomotives for their time, with 21×26in cylinders, the largest then used in the country, and 4ft 7in driving wheels.

343

There were nine of these engines, built by Messrs Beyer Peacock & Co., and after electrification in 1904 they were sold out of service, three to the Alexandra Docks Railway, eventually becoming GWR Nos 1344–1346, withdrawn in the 1920s; and two to the Shipley Collieries, Derbyshire. One of these, *Cecil Raikes* was at work until 1954, and on withdrawal was set aside for preservation. It is at the time of writing undergoing restoration at Steamtown, Southport. The remaining four were sold to a firm in Australia for industrial work.

344 On one railway at least, albeit a small one, the 0-6-4T was the principal class throughout its existence – the Sligo, Leitrim & Northern Counties Railway in Ireland. It had ten of them in all out of a total of 18 engines during its lifetime. They were all built by Beyer Peacock & Co., the first five between 1882 and 1899. These had 4ft 9in driving wheels, with 16½ × 20in cylinders. Their somewhat archaic appearance is shown by the picture of *Lissadell* taken in 1955, but they underwent practically no alteration or rebuilding, and two of them remained in service until the closure of the line in 1957. It was intended that *Hazlewood* should be preserved in Belfast museum, but unfortunately it was broken up by mistake when the scrap dealers moved in.

345

A much modernised version appeared in 1904, with two more in 1905 and 1915 (**345**). Finally, another very similar pair were built in 1949, again by Messrs Beyer Peacock, but by the time they were ready the company's finances were in such a poor state that it was unable to pay for them. They were not delivered until 1951 under a hire purchase agreement. They had the regrettable distinction of being the last new conventional steam engines for any railway in Ireland. One of them, *Lough Erne*, is preserved at the Whitehead premises of the Railway Preservation Society.

SL&NCR engines were remarkable in that they were unnumbered, and carried names only.

346 The SL&NCR engines were not quite the earliest 0-6-4Ts. The type had been originally introduced, again in Ireland, in 1876 by McDonnell on the Great Southern & Western Railway, when No 92, built in 1880, underwent conversion to an inspection coach. It was photographed at Inchicore in 1932.

344

346

347

348

349

347 Four 0-6-4Ts were built for the Great Northern of Ireland Railway in 1908 and 1911 for shunting duties at Belfast. No 167 was photographed at Belfast in 1930.

348 The one and only 0-6-4T of the Belfast & County Down Railway was built in 1923 for exchange of goods traffic between the docks and Belfast Queens Quay.

349 Again a solitary specimen, No 9 *King Edward* was built in 1904 for the 3ft 0in gauge Cavan & Leitrim Railway. It was little used as it was found to be too heavy for the line, and was scrapped in 1934.

350 The North Stafford had a small collection of 0-6-4Ts of two varieties; eight engines with 5ft 0in wheels for freight duties, built at the company's own works at Stoke in 1914–5, and another eight with 5ft 6in wheels for passenger work built between 1916 and 1919, both

350

351

352

353

series having 20 × 26in cylinders. They became LMS 2040–2055 at the grouping, but in common with all other NSR engines, all were withdrawn by 1939.

351 The last engines built for the Lancashire Derbyshire and East Coast Railway before its absorption by the GCR in 1907 were nine 0-6-4Ts, which came out in 1904 and 1906. They became GCR 1145–1153 and LNER 6145–6153, and some of them survived the war, the last being scrapped in 1947.

352 Wainwright's last design for the SE&CR was for five 0-6-4Ts built in 1913, but owing to his premature retirement because of ill health no more were constructed, as they hardly conformed to the ideas of his successor, Maunsell. As BR 31595–31599 they were scrapped during 1949–51.

353 The only Swindon-built 0-6-4Ts on the GWR were three pannier tank crane engines for shunting at Swindon and Wolverhampton works, Nos 17 *Cyclops* and 18 *Steropes* (built in 1901) together with No 16 *Hercules*, added in 1921. All were withdrawn in 1936.

354 The GWR had however inherited ten 0-6-4Ts from the Barry Railway, dating from 1914. They were apparently unsatisfactory engines, subject to frequent derailments, and although four of them were fitted with Swindon boilers, as illustrated, they were all withdrawn in 1926.

354

355

355 Four 0-6-4Ts were built for the Metropolitan by the Yorkshire Engine Company in 1915. No 94 *Lord Aberconway* was photographed in 1927 at Neasden. They became LNER 6154–6157 and were scrapped between 1943 and 1948.

These were the only named engines on the Metropolitan Railway since the early days, Nos 95–97 being *Robert H. Selbie*, *Charles Jones* and *Brill* respectively.

2-6-0

356 The 2-6-0 originated in America, where it was generally known as the Mogul. It first appeared in Britain on the Great Eastern in 1878, and it was appropriate that the first engine actually carried the name *Mogul*, one of only three engines on the GER to receive such a distinction. There were 15 of the class built by Neilsons, mainly to the design of W. Adams, who however went over to the LSWR before they were completed by his successor Mr Bromley. They had 4ft 10in wheels with 19 × 26in cylinders.

356

357

358

359

They were not particularly successful, and all were scrapped by 1887, which probably explains the lack of enthusiasm for the type shown by other locomotive engineers of the time.

357 Only two more of the type appeared before the end of the century, in 1895–7 on the small Midland & South Western Junction Railway. One of these was photographed after being sold to the Hartley Main Collieries, Northumberland, where it worked until 1943.

358 In 1899–1900 the demand for new engines was so acute that British firms were unable to accept any new orders, so recourse was made by three railways to the importation of 80 2-6-0s from the USA, from the works of Baldwins and the Schenectady Loco Co. Between them these companies supplied 40 engines for the Midland, whilst Baldwin also provided 20 each for the GNR and GCR.

All these engines had 5ft 0in driving wheels and 18 × 24in cylinders, and were an essentially American design, including the use of bar frames, universal in that country, but practically unknown in Britain since earlier days. None of them lasted very long by British standards even at that period. American practice was not geared to longevity. The life of a locomotive to a large extent was governed by the date the boiler was due for replacement. On the other hand it was British practice to rebuild, sometimes several times. Even on the Midland, a line on which most locomotives enjoyed particularly long lives, all of the Yankee 2-6-0s had gone by 1914.

359 In 1900 Dean on the GWR decided to give the 2-6-0 a tryout, in the shape of an inside-cylinder locomotive with double frames. (The initial engine was actually built as a 4-6-0.) Eventually 81 of these appeared between then and 1906, numbered 2600–2680. They had many variations of boiler and other details during their careers, but the general design remained the same. The first engines were known as Krugers, a name derived from the South African war in progress at the time, but the later engines acquired the nickname of Aberdares, as many of them worked in South Wales. They were good sturdy freight locomotives, with 4ft 7½in driving wheels and 18 × 26in cylinders. All eventually received super-heaters and piston valves. A good many of them were scrapped during the 1930s, but 12 of them just survived nationalisation after a working life of nearly 50 years.

360 Even so, the 2-6-0 still hung fire, not to be taken up with any enthusiasm until 1911, again on the GWR, when Churchward produced his own version. This engine was in his normal style, with two large outside cylinders of 18½ × 30in. The long stroke, together with piston valves of 10in diameter and 6in travel, were already standard dimensions on Churchward's larger passenger classes. These features were undoubtedly the

chief contribution to the outstanding success of his engines, but this was not realised by other locomotive engineers until several years later, and possibly not even fully by Churchward himself at the time.

The new 2-6-0s had 5ft 8in driving wheels and 200lb boiler pressure. They proved to be exceedingly useful mixed traffic engines, being used on semi-main line passenger work and on cross-country routes. In all no less than 342 of them were built up to the year 1932, with slight modifications in the later series.

A good many of the earlier ones were scrapped in the late 1930s, not long after the final ones were built. This was mainly accounted for by the decision to replace them with lightweight 4-6-0s of the Grange and Manor classes, but nevertheless 241 of them survived into nationalisation, and many of them lasted until the virtual end of steam on the Western Region in 1964. No 5322 is preserved at the Didcot Railway Centre, and 7325 (originally 9303) on the Severn Valley Railway.

361 A year after the appearance of the Churchward engines just described, Gresley produced his first 2-6-0s for the GNR. Allowing for the very different ideas of the two engineers, the designs had much in common: two outside cylinders, 5ft 8in driving wheels, and intended for the same mixed traffic range of duties. Gresley proceeded to build more 2-6-0s for the GNR and subsequently the LNER, with four varieties in all.

The first ones, the original class K1, had consisted of ten engines only with 4ft 8in diameter boilers. They were followed by class K2, 65 engines built between 1913 and 1921. These had enlarged boilers of 5ft 6in diameter, to which dimensions all of the K1s were later constructed. The K3s (illustrated), went a stage further, with an

360

1939 at Hither Green, was one of the later series of the N class (**365**). As with many modern types it was later felt desirable to fit smoke deflectors to prevent drifting steam exhaust from obscuring the driver's lookout, although for some reason this was never found to be necessary on the Irish engines.

Two other varieties of Maunsell's 2-6-0 appeared later, very similar to the Ns, but with 6ft 0in driving wheels. 50 of these were two-cylinder engines, Class U. Of these 20 were rebuilds of 2-6-4Ts Nos A790–A809, and the others were built new as 2-6-0s, Nos A610–A639. No A629 was photographed in 1932 with modified tender, when it was temporarily adapted to burn pulverised fuel, the plant of which can be seen in the illustration (**367**).

There were also 21 6ft 0in engines with three cylinders, class U1. The first of the class was a similar rebuild of 2-6-4T No A890 (see **402**), and another 20 were built as 2-6-0 tender engines, Nos A891–A900, and 1901–1910 in accordance with the renumbering scheme introduced in 1931 (**368**).

No N1s or U1s now survive, but N class No 31874 is at work on the Mid-Hants Railway bearing the name *Aznar Line*, and U class No 1618 is to be seen on the Bluebell Railway.

367

368

366

369

369 Apart from the GWR Aberdares inside-cylinder 2-6-0s were rare, but McIntosh built five for the Caledonian in 1912. They were little more than elongated

0-6-0s, the leading pony truck protruding from the front underneath an extension to the frames. Ostensibly this increased the weight distribution, but in fact 46 tons out of the total 54 tons still rested on the coupled wheels. As LMS 17800–17804 they lasted until 1935–7.

370 The G&SWR had 11 fairly similar locomotives built by Drummond in 1915. Both these and the CR engines had 5ft 0in driving wheels, with 19½ × 26in cylinders.

They became LMS 17820–17830 at the grouping and all would probably have been scrapped by 1939; four were however reprieved owing to the war, during which time they were on loan to the Highland, and these lasted until 1944–1947.

371 There were a few inside-cylinder 2-6-0s on the GS&WR in Ireland, built between 1903 and 1909. One of these, No 356, was used by Mr Bulleid as a guinea pig for his projected turf burning engine (see **565**). The conversion, which was effected in 1952, included amongst other alterations the fitting of a pair of preheating boilers, one on each side of the ordinary boiler, as seen in the photograph taken at Inchicore in 1953. There was also a mechanical stoker and an enlarged tender to accommodate the more bulky nature of the fuel. Although hardly a success on its trials it provided much useful experience in connection with the actual design of the ultimate turf burning engine which eventually appeared in 1957. The experimental loco was scrapped in the same year.

372 The Dublin & South Eastern also had a couple of inside-cylinder 2-6-0s, built in 1922, Nos 461 and 462, of which the first has been preserved in its original state as DSER No 15.

370

371

372

373 The LMS (NCC) adopted the 2-6-0 for its express services in 1933. With obvious Midland features, the first four, Nos 90–93 were in fact built at Derby; the remainder, Nos 94–104, although using boilers supplied by Derby, were actually constructed at Belfast between 1934 and 1942. With 6ft 0in driving wheels they were fast runners and performed adequately on the Londonderry expresses until their withdrawal in the 1960s owing to dieselisation.

373

374

374 Hughes of the L&YR was the first loco superintendent of the LMS and he was responsible for the new 2-6-0s which appeared in 1926, although he had by that time been replaced by Fowler. With their high running plates they were somewhat revolutionary for the time, but were a definite pointer to the future trend of locomotive design. This gave rise at the time to the nickname of

Spiders, but more recently they were generally known as Crabs. With 5ft 6in driving wheels they were definitely mixed traffic engines although they did very good main line passenger work on the Highland during the early 1930s.

There were in all 245 of them, LMS Nos 13000–13244, later 2700–2944, and finally BR 42700–42944. The original 2700 is preserved in the NRM at York.

Stanier produced a modified version with a taper boiler in 1933. These engines, LMS Nos 2945–2984, eventually became BR Nos 42945–42984 (**375**). No 2968 survives on the Severn Valley Railway.

375

376

376 Among the last new pre-nationalisation designs to appear before the 1948 amalgamation were two varieties of 2-6-0 by H. G. Ivatt, on the LMS. The smaller ones, class 2, with 5ft 0in wheels, 16 × 24in cylinders and 200lb pressure, consisted of 20 engines built at Crewe in 1946–7, Nos 6400–6419. Subsequent additions during the early years of nationalisation brought them to a total of 128, BR Nos 46400–46527.

378

377

377 The larger class 4 variety had 5ft 3in wheels, 18 × 28in cylinders and 225lb pressure. Only the first three came out as LMS engines, the following engines being painted in BR style from the start. The extremely high apology for a running plate, together with their double chimneys (later replaced with single blast pipes) made them about the ugliest engines ever to appear on the LMS. A total of 162 engines were built, Nos 43000–43161.

378 Under the BR nationalisation scheme both of the Ivatt 2-6-0s were perpetuated by Riddles as standard types with a few modifications, and certainly some

379

improvement in appearance. The 43000s were followed by the 76000 class in 1955, Nos 76000–76114.

The 78000s, also introduced in 1953, were very similar to the 46400s, and were numbered 78000–78054 (**379**).

There was also an intermediate 5ft 3in 77000 class, classified 3, again with an unnecessarily high running plate for such a small wheel (**380**). It cannot be any cause for regret that none of these 20 engines, Nos 77000–77019, have survived.

There are however several examples of the other class 2 and 4 LMS and BR engines still to be seen. 46464 and 46512 are preserved on the Strathspey Railway; 46441 (in LMS lake as 6441) at Steamtown, Carnforth; 46443, 46521 and 43106 on the Severn Valley; 78022 on the Keighley & Worth Valley; 76017 on the Mid Hants; and others in the process of restoration.

380

381

382

2-6-0T

For some reason the 2-6-0T has never been adopted by any of the major railway companies. It is hard to understand why, as it would seem to be a neat handy type for the sort of purpose for which 0-6-2Ts, 0-4-4Ts and 2-4-2Ts have been so widely employed. Such specimens as have appeared, with one exception, have all been one-off designs.

381 The nearest approach to a 2-6-0T on a main line British railway was No 777, one of Webb's uncoupled compound experiments, and strictly speaking a 2-(2-4)-0T. Built in 1877, this engine had 5ft 2½in driving wheels, two outside high-pressure cylinders of 14 × 24in, and a single 30 × 24in inside cylinder. The type was not perpetuated, and No 777 was scrapped in 1899.

382 In 1909 a 2-6-0T was built for the Garstang & Knott End Railway. *Blackpool* eventually became LMS No 11680, and was finally scrapped in 1927.

383

383 Wrexham Mold & Connah's Quay No 3 was built in 1901, and had 4ft 8in driving wheels and 16 × 24in cylinders. It became GCR No 400B, but was scrapped after a very short life in 1907.

384

384 The 3ft 0in gauge Tralee & Dingle in Ireland had seven 2-6-0Ts, dating back to 1889. No 8 was photographed at Tralee in 1934.

385 Built in 1880 for the 3ft 0in gauge Ballymena & Larne Railway, NCC No 109 had 3ft 3in driving wheels and 14 × 18in cylinders. It was scrapped in 1932.

386 Castlederg & Victoria Bridge No 4 was built in 1904. It was sold to the Clogher Valley Railway in 1934, and converted to a 2-6-2T (see **400**).

386

385

2-6-2

387 The only 2-6-2 tender engine in this country prior to the grouping was an experimental multi-cylinder locomotive built at Derby in 1908 for the Midland Railway. Although R. M. Deeley was CME at the time, it was designed by Cecil Paget the General Superintendent. It had eight 18 × 12in cylinders in two groups of four, all mounted inside between the driving axles. The

387

centre axle had four cranks and the fore and aft axles had two. To allow sufficient room for the width of the cylinder castings and the motion, outside frames had to be used. The driving wheels were 5ft 4in and the boiler, with a pressure of 180lb, had a large firebox of maximum possible width extending over the frames.

The engine ran a few trial trips and it was said to be powerful and fast, reputedly attaining a maximum speed of 82 mph. The sleeve valves however gave a lot of trouble with leakage, and the engine was laid aside for several years in Derby works covered with sheeting, no visitors being allowed near it. It became almost a legend to the railway students of the time, as no details or drawings were released until some time after it had been quietly cut up in 1919. The illustration of No 2299, as it was numbered, is the official view of the engine, the only known photograph of it in existence.

388 The only other 2-6-2s, or Prairies as they were sometimes known, to run in Britain were Gresley's designs for the LNER. The first engine, the well known *Green Arrow*, No 4771, appeared in 1936; it was followed by many more right through the war years until 1944, by which time they totalled 184. They might be described as

express mixed traffic engines, but they were rather more than that in that they could, and did, work alongside Pacifics on top link duties. They were found to be a godsend for the heavy traffic on the east coast main line during the war years, being able to tackle trains of 20 coaches or more. This was no doubt the reason why their continued production was allowed during those difficult times.

These engines had three cylinders of 18½ × 26in, 6ft 2in driving wheels, and 220lb pressure. The original *Green Arrow* herself is part of the NRM collection, maintained in working order, and frequently to be seen on enthusiasts' specials in the north of England.

388

389 A lightweight version was intended for general use on the LNER, but only two were built before Gresley's death in 1941, and his successor Thompson did not continue construction. These smaller 2-6-2s, which had three 15 × 26in cylinders and 5ft 8in wheels, were No 3401 *Bantam Cock* and No 3402, which although not officially named, inevitably became known as *Bantam Hen*. One was tried out initially on the Great Eastern

389

section, but both soon gravitated to Scotland. As BR 61700 and 61701 they lasted until 1957.

2-6-2T

390 The Mersey Railway, opened in 1886, which was a very early user of the 0-6-4T (see **343**), was actually the first company to introduce the 2-6-2T to this country in 1887. There were nine such engines, as in the case of the 0-6-4Ts, and they were likewise sold out of service on electrification in 1903. Seven went to the Alexandra Docks Railway, later to be absorbed into the GWR system; the other two went to collieries. The Alexandra Docks added two more of much the same design in 1920. The photograph shows No 13 *Brunlees*, later Alexandra Docks No 10 and eventually GWR 1201. It was scrapped in 1929.

391 20 2-6-2Ts were built by H. A. Hoy for the Lancashire & Yorkshire in 1903–4, intended as enlargements of the 2-4-2Ts for heavy suburban work. They had 5ft 8in driving wheels and 19 × 26in cylinders. They were in fact a dismal failure, unpopular from the start, prone to rough riding and even derailment. After 1913 they were withdrawn from passenger work and put on

banking duties. Only 17 survived the grouping and the last of them was withdrawn in 1926.

The Great Western made considerable use of the 2-6-2T, both for suburban working and cross-country and branch lines. First introduced by Churchward in 1902, there were broadly three classes, with driving wheels of 5ft 8in, 4ft 7½in, and 4ft 1½in. The last mentioned, the 4400 class, consisted of 11 engines only, built in 1904 for more hilly routes such as the Princetown branch; they had all disappeared by 1955.

390

391

153

392

393

394

Group, 4160 with the Standard Gauge Steam Trust, Tyseley, and two or three others in process of restoration.

The GWR also had 20 inside-cylinder 2-6-2Ts, which were rather curious conversions from 0-6-0 tender engines.

394 On the LMS Fowler introduced the 2-6-2T in 1930 for general suburban and branch line work, some in the London area being fitted with condensing apparatus, as illustrated by No 40, photographed at St Pancras in 1938. They had 5ft 3in driving wheels and 17½ × 26in

392 The 4ft 7½in engines, the 4500 class, which were introduced in 1906 for general purpose duties, eventually totalled 175 examples and several of these have survived into the preservation age. Nos 4555 and 4588, for instance, are to be found at work on the Dart Valley Railway or its subsidiary, the Torbay and Dartmouth, and others are to be seen on the Severn Valley, West Somerset and at other locations.

393 The larger 5ft 8in engines, some of which were later reconstructed or rebuilt with 5ft 3in wheels under the Collett regime, conformed in general more to Churchward's standard dimensions of 18 × 30in cylinders and 200–225lb boiler pressure for main line passenger engines. The last ones to be built did not actually appear until the end of 1949, two years after nationalisation, by which time many of the earlier examples had already been scrapped. Some of these later engines inevitably had short lives, 1965 seeing the end of steam on the Western region, but a few have survived at preservation centres: 6106 at Didcot, 4141 and 5164 on the Severn Valley, 4110 by the GWR Preservation cylinders. Originally Nos 15500–15569, they later became LMS Nos 1–70.

Stanier followed them up with his own version of generally similar dimensions but with taper boilers, but although of nominally the same tractive effort these engines always seemed to be inferior to their predecessors. They were Nos 71–209, eventually becoming BR 40071–40209. The last of both classes went in 1962.

395 In 1946 H. A. Ivatt produced a new lightweight 2-6-2T, which proved to be an excellent engine in every way. Some of the class were fitted with push-pull apparatus. They had 5ft 0in driving wheels and 16 or 16½ × 24in cylinders. The first ten came out as LMS engines, Nos 1200–1209, to be followed after nationalisation by Nos 41210–41329.

No 41241 survives on the Keighley & Worth Valley Railway, and one or two more are under restoration at other preservation centres.

The design was adopted in 1953 as one of the 12 standard types for further construction, and 30 were built, Nos 84000–84029. There was also a new, slightly larger type with 5ft 3in driving wheels, and 17½ × 26in cylinders, Nos 82000–82044.

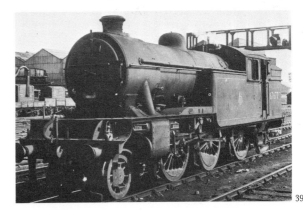

396

396 On the LNER, Gresley's three-cylinder 2-6-2Ts appeared in 1930. They were initially intended for the Metropolitan widened lines and Kings Cross suburban routes, although in fact they never worked on the GNR lines around London. Some did see service on the Great Eastern, but the majority of them went to the North Eastern and to Scotland, where they almost monopolised the busy Glasgow and Edinburgh suburban services. There were eventually 92 of them in all, built between 1930 and 1940. The last ten had the boiler pressure raised from 180lb to 200lb, and were classified V3, the earlier ones being V1 (V2 and V4 were Gresley's 2-6-2 tender engines). The driving wheels were 5ft 8in, and they had cylinders of 16 × 26in. They eventually became BR 67600–67691, all being scrapped between 1960 and 1964.

395

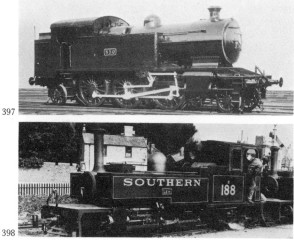

397

398

narrow gauge line the Southern inherited at the grouping. It was regrettably a very early closure (September 1935) in comparison with other such light railways in this country. The engines had been built by Manning Wardle, three in 1897 and the fourth in 1925. The first three, numbered by the Southern Railway, were 759 *Yeo*, 760 *Exe*, and 761 *Tawe*. The later engine was No 188 *Lew*, and this one was sold on closure of the line and sent to Brazil.

They had driving wheels of 2ft 10in, 10½ × 16in cylinders and a boiler pressure of 160lb.

399 On the Irish narrow gauge system there were 2-6-2Ts on the Tralee & Dingle (one only, now preserved in the USA), West Clare (four), and also a single specimen on the Clogher Valley Railway. Photographed at Aughnacloy in 1937, the latter was a rebuild from a 2-6-0T obtained from the Castlederg & Victoria Bridge Railway when that line closed in 1934 (see **386**).

397 There was only one standard gauge 2-6-2T in Ireland, built for the Great Southern in 1928 and intended mainly for the boat train between Dublin and Dun Laoghaire, although it does not seem to have been very popular on that duty. No 850 had 5ft 6in wheels, 17½ × 28in cylinders and 160lb pressure. It was scrapped in 1955.

398 Four out of the five engines of the 2ft 0in gauge Lynton & Barnstaple Railway were 2-6-2Ts, and they were unique in several respects. They were the only engines of this wheel arrangement on the Southern Railway, and the Lynton & Barnstaple was the only

399

400 The 1ft 11½in gauge Vale of Rheidol Railway is now the only part of the BR system still steam worked. There are three 2-6-2Ts: No 7 *Owain Glyndwr*; No 8 *Llywelyn*, built in 1923; and No 9 *Prince of Wales*, built in 1902 and one of the railway's original engines. The driving wheels were 2ft 6in, and the cylinders 11½ × 17in, with 160lb pressure. The line operates from Aberystwyth to Devils Bridge during the summer season only.

2-6-4T

401 There was never a 2-6-4 tender engine in Britain, and the 2-6-4T did not make an appearance until 1914, when Robinson on the Great Central produced such a design with inside cylinders. All subsequent engines of the type on other railways had outside cylinders.

20 engines in all were built between 1914 and 1917. They were employed mainly on goods work, but are known to have worked passenger trains on occasion between Rickmansworth and Aylesbury and in the Nottingham area. All were withdrawn between 1947 and 1955.

402 In 1917 Maunsell produced his 2-6-4T concurrently with his 2-6-0 (see **365**). No 790 was intended for express duties on the SE & CR main line. It had 6ft 0in driving wheels and 19 × 26in cylinders. Owing to the war, there was a delay in production of any further examples, but eventually 19 more appeared in 1925–6 and another odd one with three cylinders. All, including the original, were named after rivers, and consequently became known as the River class, Nos A790–A809; and A890, *River Frome*, the three-cylinder engine.

The Sevenoaks accident of 20 August 1927 put paid to their careers. No 800 *River Cray* was derailed at speed

400

401

402

157

with disastrous results. All of the engines were immediately taken out of service pending enquiry, and although it was established that the fault lay with poor track and ballast rather than the design of the engine, all were converted to 2-6-0 tender engines.

In spite of this another 15 2-6-4Ts incorporating the tanks and other parts of the converted engines appeared in 1931, with 5ft 6in wheels and three 16½ × 28in cylinders. These were intended strictly for freight work, and under no circumstances were they to be used on passenger trains, a restriction which applied throughout their existence. All lasted until the 1960s (**403**).

403

404 The last new steam engines built for the Metropolitan Railway were six 2-6-4Ts delivered in 1924. Nos 111–116 were designed mainly for the coal traffic to Neasden power station from the Midlands, where it was handed over from the LMS to the Met. system at Verney Junction. They incorporated spare parts of the Maunsell 2-6-0s built at Woolwich in 1924–5 (see **365**).

No 116 was photographed at Neasden after it had been transferred to London Transport in 1936. In 1937 the engines became LNER 6158–6163. All were scrapped by 1948.

404

405 Notwithstanding the unfortunate experience of the Southern Railway, Fowler had no hesitation in proceeding with the production of his own design of 2-6-4T for general passenger use on the LMS, already well under way in 1927. His engines were destined to be the forerunners of a long series to be perpetuated with some modifications by Stanier and Fairburn (**406**), and finally Riddles on the BR after nationalisation (**407**).

405

406

The original Fowler engines had 5ft 9in driving wheels, 19 × 26in cylinders and 200lb pressure. These dimensions broadly applied to all of the later engines, the final BR ones having 5ft 8in wheels, 18 × 28in cylinders and 225lb pressure. The chief difference in those built by

407

Stanier and his successors was the provision of a taper boiler, and he also produced 37 engines with three 16 × 26in cylinders in 1934 especially for the Tilbury section.

The whole series can best be summed up as follows:

BR Nos 42300–42424 Original Fowler engines with parallel boiler
42425–42495 and 42537–42672 Stanier two-cylinder locos
42500–42536 Stanier three-cylinder locos
42673–42699, 42050–42299 Fairburn two-cylinder locos (last one built 1950)
80000–80154 Riddles standard BR design, built 1952–1957

The preservation position regarding the LMS engines is poor. None of the original Fowlers survive, and there are only two Fairburns on the Lakeside Railway and the first of the Stanier three-cylinder engines, No 2500, at Bressingham Hall on loan from the National Collection.

Several of the BR ones survive, however, at the time of writing. They include 80002 on the K&WVR, 80064 on the Dart Valley, 80079 on the Severn Valley, 80100 on the Bluebell, 80105 with the Scottish Preservation Society, 80125 on the North Yorkshire Moors railway, and 80151 on the Stour Valley. Others may possibly be restored in the future.

408 Although the original engines have all disappeared, there is a near equivalent to the Fowlers still in existence. The type was adopted in 1946 for use on the NCC in Northern Ireland, the only difference from the originals being in the use of 6ft 0in driving wheels. 18

408

409

410

were built at Derby, the last in 1950, Nos 1–10 and 50–57. They were at work until the end of steam on the Ulster Transport Authority in the late 1960s.

No 4 has been secured by the Irish Railway Preservation Society and is used on occasional rail tours organised by that Society all over Ireland.

409 Thompson introduced the 2-6-4T to the LNER with one engine in 1945, No 9000; another 99 followed between 1948 and 1950, all except the first few being turned out in BR livery. They had 20 × 26in cylinders and 5ft 2in driving wheels, rather small for some of the semi-fast main line duties they performed, such as buffet car expresses between Kings Cross and Cambridge, and over the lengthier sections on the Metropolitan line between Rickmansworth and Aylesbury. They eventually became BR 67701–67800, and all were scrapped between 1960 and 1962.

410 Two narrow gauge 2-6-4Ts were built for the Leek & Manifold Valley Light Railway, a subsidiary of the North Stafford which opened in 1904 and closed in 1934. Although they became LMS engines, they were never actually renumbered into its stock. They were No 1 *E. R. Calthrop* and No 2 *J. B. Earle*, built by Kitsons in 1904.

411

411 In Ireland, there were eight 2-6-4Ts on the 3ft 0in gauge County Donegal Railway, its principal type in its last years. One of these, No 2 *Blanche*, is in Belfast Museum. Another, No 6 *Columbkille*, is at Londonderry, the property of the recently formed North West of Ireland Society, which hopes to reopen a short length of line along the site of the railway in that city. The two engines were built by Nasmyth Wilson in 1912 and 1907 respectively.

412

413

4-6-0

412 The 4-6-0 design made its first appearance in Great Britain on the Highland in 1894, when 15 engines appeared to the design of David Jones, Nos 103–117. With 5ft 3in driving wheels, and 20 × 26in cylinders, they were intended primarily for goods work, but were often pressed into passenger service during the summer season when the resources of the locomotive department were strained to the utmost.

They underwent little change during their lifetime, some losing their smokebox wing plates and acquiring Drummond type chimneys in place of the unique louvre design much favoured by David Jones. This had an inner barrel encased by an outer one with a series of vents on the front side. It was an early device to obtain an upward current of air, lifting the exhaust clear of the driver's view. This problem was encountered to an increasing degree many years later with some larger-boilered modern designs, and the ultimate remedy was found to be the use of deflectors at the side of the smokebox, familiar on many more recent designs.

All of the Jones goods survived the grouping to become LMS 17916–17930, being withdrawn during the 1930s. The original engine, No 103, was set aside for preservation on withdrawal in 1934. Restored to original condition, it was put into working order in 1959 and for a time used on rail tour specials. It is now in Glasgow museum, the only Highland engine still in existence.

413 Peter Drummond succeeded David Jones in 1896 and in 1900 he brought out a passenger 4-6-0 for the Highland. This was the Castle class, with 5ft 9in wheels, 19 of which were built between 1900 and 1917. They bore the brunt of express working over the HR main line for many years. They became LMS 14675–14693, and some of them survived the Second World War, the last one, No 14690 *Dalcross Castle* lasting until 1947. It is interesting to note that 50 identical engines were built by British makers for the Western Railway of France in 1911. These disappeared during the 1930s.

414   The year 1899 also saw the first express 4-6-0s in England, ten engines built by Wilson Worsdell for the NER. They had 6ft 0in driving wheels, and were later relegated to mixed traffic duties, but five more came out in 1900 with 6ft 8¼in wheels, and these remained on express passenger work until their withdrawal in 1929–1931. Nevertheless, although 4-6-0s continued to appear on the NER until 1924 these later engines were mainly for mixed traffic duties. The NER, together with its co-partners on the east coast route to Scotland the GNR and NBR, remained essentially an Atlantic line. The only other railways to come into the LNER at the grouping employing 4-6-0s were the GCR and GER.

414

415

415   The first main line to adopt the 4-6-0 on a really large scale for express passenger work was the Great Western. Discounting a couple of double-framed inside-cylinder engines built by William Dean in 1896 and 1901, which formed the basis of the Aberdare 2-6-0s already described, the first express 4-6-0 saw the light of day in 1902. Designed by G. J. Churchward, it was destined to be the forerunner of a long line of distinctive engines. With its high running plate and large domeless boiler it presented a somewhat startling appearance at the time, but set the pattern for the individuality of future GWR locomotives.

The first engine was No 100, later to become 2900 *William Dean*. It had what were to become standard Churchward dimensions for two-cylinder express engines: 18 × 30in cylinders (later increased to 18½ × 30in), 200lb pressure, and 6ft 8½in driving wheels. Nos 98 and 171 followed in 1903, and the latter ran experimentally as an Atlantic for a few years between 1904 and 1907. Some further engines were built to this wheel arrangement, but all were subsequently converted to 4-6-0s.

The class eventually totalled 77 engines, Nos 2900–2955, 2971–2990 and 2998 (the original 98). They were named in batches of Ladies, Saints and Courts (illustrated); 2971–2998 had miscellaneous names. The class as a whole was however generally known as the Saints. The last survivor, No 2920 *Saint David* was scrapped in 1953.

416

416 The first four-cylinder engine was No 40, built in 1906 as an Atlantic, but later to become the prototype four-cylinder 4-6-0, No 4000 *North Star*. It was followed by another 72 engines, 4001–4072 between 1907 and 1923, named after Stars, Knights, Kings (later to become Monarchs) Queens, Princes, Princesses and Abbeys. They had the usual 6ft 8½in driving wheels and four 14¼ × 26in cylinders. No 4003 *Lode Star* is preserved in Swindon Museum.

417 In 1924 Collett produced an improved version with some increase in dimensions, notably to the cylinders which were enlarged to 16 × 26in. These, the Castles, were probably the best known of all GWR 4-6-0s. They were built up to 1950 and the class eventually totalled 171, a few of which were rebuilds of Stars. They carried the numbers 111, which was a rebuild of

The Great Bear (see **464**), 4000, 4009, 4016, 4032, 4037, 4073–4099, 5000–5099, and 7000–7037, (5083–5092 were rebuilds of 4063–4072). The last one was appropriately named *Great Western*.

Their ability to handle heavy trains at sustained high speeds was most impressive, and they remained on top link express duties until replaced by diesels in the early 1960s. A few have been preserved, notably the original, 4073 *Caerphilly Castle* in South Kensington museum, and 4079 *Pendennis Castle*, which finally went to Australia. Others at the Didcot Railway Centre and the Standard Gauge Steam Trust, Birmingham are scheduled for restoration to running condition.

417

418

163

418 The ultimate in GWR 4-6-0 design was the well known King class, 30 engines built in 1927. These had 6ft 6in driving wheels, four 16¼ × 28in cylinders, and 250lb pressure. The original 6000 *King George V* is preserved in working order at Bulmer's, Hereford, and is sometimes to be seen on main line steam specials, whilst 6024 *King Edward I* is at the time of writing undergoing restoration at Quainton Road.

419 The Hall class was a two-cylinder general mixed traffic engine, the original, No 4900 *Saint Martin*, being a rebuild in 1924 of Saint class No 2925. They had 6ft 0in driving wheels and standard 18½ × 30in cylinders. 329 further engines built between 1928 and 1950, Nos 4901–4999, 5900–5999, 6900–6999 and 7900–7929, all named after Halls. Several are preserved at various locations.

420 The Grange class had 5ft 8in driving wheels, but were otherwise similar to the Halls. 80 engines, Nos 6800–6879, were built between 1926 and 1939, mainly to replace 2-6-0s of the 4300 class.

The Manor class was a lighter version of the Grange suitable for working over lines of restricted route availability such as the Cambrian. 30 engines, Nos 7800–7829, were built between 1938 and 1950. They are a popular type for preservation societies, for which several have been secured for restoration to working order.

421 The County class was the last new variant of GWR 4-6-0. 30 engines, Nos 1000–1029, were built by Hawksworth between 1945 and 1947. They had 6ft 3in driving wheels, two 18½ × 30in cylinders and a pressure of 280lb. Apart from a single elongated splasher in place of individual ones they conformed to the long established conventions of GWR practice. They perpetuated many of the names formerly carried by Churchward's last design of 4-4-0.

They were never very popular engines, falling as they did rather uncomfortably between express and mixed traffic classification.

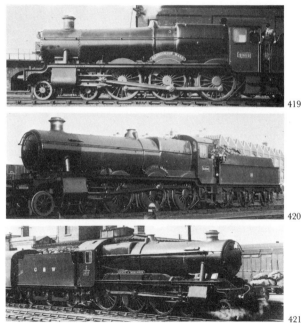

419

420

421

422 The LNWR was a large user of 4-6-0s in later years. For goods work there were initially 30 four-cylinder compounds, Webb's last design, which came out in 1903–5 just after his retirement. They were poor engines, slow, sluggish and unreliable. All were broken up by 1920.

423 Whale introduced a much better version in 1906, with two inside cylinders. This class was known as the 19 inch goods, the cylinder dimensions being 19 × 26in; they had 5ft 2¼in wheels. The 170 engines eventually

became LMS 8700–8869. Some later received Belpaire fireboxes, and the last one went in 1946.

424 Whale's 4-6-0 express engines were initiated by No 66 *Experiment* which appeared in 1905. These also had inside 19 × 26in cylinders, but the driving wheel diameter was 6ft 3in. 105 of them were built between 1905 and 1910. They were allocated LMS 5450–5554 but all were scrapped before the Second World War.

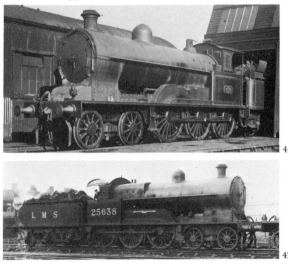

425 Bowen Cooke produced a superheated version of the Experiment in 1911, the Prince of Wales class, of which there were 245 by 1921. They became LMS 5600–5844, later engines being renumbered by the addition of 20000. Many of them received Belpaire fireboxes. They were excellent engines and took a large share in main line working on the LNWR, handling trains far heavier than those of today.

An additional engine, No 5845 of the Prince of Wales class, was equipped with outside valve gear, giving it the appearance of an outside-cylinder engine, which it was not. It was built in 1924 for the Wembley Exhibition. Four others were similarly converted (**426**). A few Princes just managed to survive nationalisation in 1948, but not long enough to carry a BR number, let alone be preserved.

427

426

427 The Claughtons, Bowen Cooke's four-cylinder engines, were distinguished by their deep framing, giving them a somewhat massive appearance. The first came out in 1913, and by 1921 there were 130 of them, LMS Nos 5900–6029. They had 6ft 9in driving wheels, four 16 × 26in cylinders, and were built new with Belpaire

428

fireboxes. In 1928 20 of them were rebuilt with larger boilers, some with Caprotti valve gear (**428**).

Although they did good work in their early years, they somehow never eclipsed the two-cylinder Princes and the George the Fifth 4-4-0s on express work, and all but two were withdrawn by the end of the 1930s. Curiously the last survivor, No 6004, outlived the rest by eight years, being withdrawn in 1949.

429 There were 19 G&SWR 4-6-0s of one class, built by Manson between 1903 and 1911. They had two outside cylinders and became LMS 14658–14674. Like most other engines of that railway they all disappeared before the war, in this case as early as 1933.

430 The Caledonian 4-6-0s comprised engines built between 1902 and 1922 under the superintendencies of McIntosh and Pickersgill, of nine widely differing varieties. The most famous of these were the seven Cardeans, inside-cylinder express engines with 6ft 6in driving wheels built between 1903 and 1912. One of these, No 907, was involved in the disastrous Quintinshill accident of 1915 and damaged beyond repair, but the others survived to become LMS 14750–14755, although withdrawn from service by 1933.

There were other varieties of the same general design, including nine engines with 5ft 3in wheels built between 1902 and 1905, specially for the hilly Oban line; five others with 5ft 0in wheels for express goods; and some for mixed traffic with 5ft 9in wheels (**431**).

431

429

430

432 Pickersgill's engines, built from 1916 onwards, had outside cylinders. Again there were only a few of each type, but one design was perpetuated after the grouping by the construction of a further 20 examples in 1925–6, and many of these survived nationalisation as 54630–54654, the last going in 1953.

A more modern class, again built specially for the Oban line, were Nos 14619–14626; there were also four three-cylinder engines for express goods, Nos 14800–14803.

433

434

and 1921. A class of 6ft 0in engines were built for express passenger work. These engines, the Clans, later became LMS 14762–14769.

A 5ft 3in version was built for mixed traffic, unnamed but generally known as the Clan goods; most of these lasted to become BR 57950–57957.

The Great Central was in a somewhat similar position to the Caledonian, although in this case the engines were the work of one designer only, J. G. Robinson. Again they were of nine different classes, each only small in number, and constructed over approximately the same period. Like the CR a mixture of outside- and inside-cylinder engines were designed, with considerable differences in appearance. They may be briefly divided into three periods, 1902–1906, 1912–1915 and 1917–1924.

435 The first group consisted of outside-cylinder locomotives, of which two engines, class B1, with 6ft 9in driving wheels, were very similar to the Atlantics and were in fact a six-coupled version built for comparative purposes. This policy paralleled that of their GWR contemporaries, but in the case of the GCR neither type was ever converted to the other. They were Nos 195 and 196, and were scrapped in 1947.

433 The River class were designed for the Highland in 1915 but taken over by the Caledonian as they were found to be too heavy for the line. After the grouping however they were transferred to the railway for which they had been originally intended. The six engines became LMS 14756–14761.

434 Reverting to the Highland, mention should be made of its last engines, all 4-6-0s, designed by Cumming. Eight each of two designs were built between 1918

435

Classes B5 and B9 were similar engines, but with 6ft 1in and 5ft 3in driving wheels for mixed traffic duties. All were withdrawn between 1944 and 1950.

436 The second group, B2 and B8, built 1912–15, had inside cylinders. Six engines of the Sam Fay class were constructed with 6ft 9in wheels for express passenger service; No 426 *City of Chester* is illustrated as running in 1921, temporarily fitted for oil burning.

A goods version with 5ft 7in wheels, the Glenalmond class comprised 11 engines built between 1913 and 1915. All of these were scrapped between 1945 and 1949.

The third GCR group, built between 1917 and 1924, reverted to outside cylinders. Class B6, three engines only, were built with 5ft 7in wheels for mixed traffic duties.

Class B7 was a four-cylinder version of the B6; they were the most numerous of GCR 4-6-0s, 28 in all, of which the last ten came out after the grouping. They had 5ft 8in wheels and four 16 × 26in cylinders. All of them survived nationalisation, but all were withdrawn quickly, the last in 1950.

437

437 Class B3 was an express version of the B7, with similar dimensions except for 6ft 9in driving wheels. They were called the Lord Faringdons. Six engines were built, of which four later received Caprotti valve gear, and one was completely rebuilt with two cylinders and a high running plate, much resembling a Thompson B1. Nevertheless this engine only lasted until 1949, the others having gone by 1947. The main reason for the rapid demise of GCR 4-6-0s was the construction of large numbers of Thompson's B1s.

The illustration shows No 6165 *Valour*, the Great Central's War Memorial engine.

438 The GER was somewhat comparable to the G&SWR, in that its 71 engines were all of one basic design, introduced by Holden in 1911. Many of them were however considerably modified by Gresley in later years in several respects, including the substitution of larger round-topped boilers and raised running plates, doing away with Holden's elaborate framing. In fact the last ten engines, Nos 8571–8580 were built new in 1928, several years after the grouping, to this design.

436

438

The original GER numbers were 1500–1570, but No 1506 had a very short life, being damaged beyond repair in an accident in 1912. Most of the class were scrapped in the 1950s.

The last survivor, No 8572, worked until 1961, when it was purchased for preservation by the North Norfolk Railway at Sheringham.

439 In 1928 Gresley introduced a 4-6-0 for main line work on routes which could not take a Pacific, notably

the GER system. These were the Sandringhams, named after stately homes in England. They had 6ft 8in driving wheels and three 17½ × 26in cylinders. 73 engines in all were built between 1928 and 1937, Nos 2800–2871. The later ones were named after football teams.

Some were later rebuilt by Thompson with two cylinders and in 1937 Nos 2859 and 2871 were streamlined on the lines of the A4 Pacifics for working the *East Anglian* express between London and Norwich.

The last survivors went in 1960.

440 The last design of LNER 4-6-0 was introduced by Thompson in 1942. Built in considerable numbers, they were general purpose engines comparable with the LMS Black 5s and the GWR Halls. By 1950 there were 410 of them, BR 61000–61409. All lasted until the 1960s, some almost to the end of steam working. Two have been preserved, Nos 1264 and 1306 *Mayflower*, both at the GCR Main Line Steam Trust, Loughborough.

439

440

441

441 Whatever success Drummond may have had on the LSWR with his 4-4-0s, his 4-6-0s were a poor lot. Nos 330–335 came out in 1904–5, and ten more of much the same pattern were built in 1908, Nos 448–457. These were all four-cylinder engines, with 6ft 0in driving wheels, intended mainly for use between Salisbury and Exeter.

Among their various defects was the fact that the outside cylinders were bolted on to the middle of the main frames, the stress on which resulted in constant fractures. No 335 was completely rebuilt by Urie in 1914 on the lines of his own engines introduced in that year, and Nos 330–334 were similarly treated in 1924. Nos 448–457 were broken up in 1925 with the exception of 449, which was used as experimental guinea pig with cranks set at 135 degrees to give eight exhaust beats per revolution of the driving wheels, in anticipation of the construction of the Lord Nelsons.

442 Drummond's last design of 4-6-0 was some improvement, ten 6ft 7in engines for express work to Salis-

bury and Bournemouth. These were Nos 443–447 and 458–462, and were built in 1911–12. Again they had four cylinders, but this time with the cylinder casing combined with the smokebox, resulting in a somewhat cumbersome appearance.

No 458 was destroyed by bomb damage at Nine Elms in October 1940; the others remained in traffic until 1948–51. No 458 was photographed in 1930 as superheated and with the firebox water tubes removed, but still retaining the somewhat clumsy splashers, which were later replaced by Maunsell with a higher running plate.

Robert Urie succeeded Drummond in 1912, and soon got down to the job of producing a workable design of 4-6-0, very different from his predecessor's efforts. With two outside cylinders only, they had the dubious distinction of being the first large-wheeled engines to have the running plates raised to a sufficient height as to be able to dispense almost entirely with splashers. They were the forerunners of a new fashion which gradually spread to other railways and was carried to extremes in the BR standard designs.

442

443 Urie's first engines, later known as class H15, had 6ft 0in wheels, 21 × 28in cylinders and 180lb pressure. Nos 482–491 came out in 1914, followed by the rebuilds of Drummond engines already mentioned and by Nos 473–478 and 521–524 in 1924.

443

444

444 The class N15, a corresponding express design with 6ft 7in wheels, Nos 736–755, came out between 1918 and 1923. The first of the true King Arthurs, Maunsell's version of Urie's 1918 design, appeared during 1925. Nos 448–457 were followed by 763–806 up to 1927, all named after knights of the Round Table. The original Urie engines were incorporated into the class and given names associated with the West Country. No 30744 *Maid of Astolat* was one of these. They did much fine work, not only in their own territory, but also on the South Eastern & Chatham main lines, until they were displaced on top link work by Bulleid's Pacifics. No 30777, a Maunsell engine, is preserved as part of the NRM collection.

445 A goods version of class H15 with 5ft 7in wheels, class S15, came out in 1920 and 1921; they were given Nos 496–515. One of these, No 506, is preserved in working order on the Mid Hants Railway, the only Urie engine still in existence.

Maunsell added to the class with the construction of Nos 823–847, built between 1927 and 1936, of which

445

No 841 can now be seen at work on the North Yorkshire Moors Railway and No 847 on the Bluebell Railway.

446 So far Maunsell's 4-6-0s had been little more than developments of Urie's designs, but in 1926 he produced a completely new class with four cylinders, for use on the Continental boat trains between Victoria and Dover. The first one, No 850 *Lord Nelson*, was followed by another 15 in 1928–9, Nos 851–865, all named after sea lords.

A few varied in detail, but the normal dimensions were 6ft 7in driving wheels, four 16½ × 26in cylinders, and 220lb pressure. No 860 *Lord Hawke*, photographed at Nine Elms in 1930, had a slightly longer boiler, but the class as a whole must surely rank among the most handsome of the many very fine 4-6-0 designs ever built. They were later fitted with steam deflectors, and ultimately with double blast pipes which necessitated an ugly wide chimney, with disastrous effect on their good looks.

A unique feature of the design was the 135 degree setting of the cranks, which gave eight beats to each revolution of the driving wheels in place of the normal four (or six with some three cylinder engines) resulting in a very quiet and even exhaust.

These fine engines lasted until 1961–2, and the original *Lord Nelson* has been preserved as part of the NRM collection, and is at the time of writing to be found at Steamtown, Carnforth.

To turn to Ireland briefly, there were in all only 22 4-6-0s ever to run in that country. All on the GS&WR, there were initially five inside-cylinder engines with 5ft 1½in wheels for goods work, built by Coey in 1905–7. Ten

446

express engines with four 14 × 26in cylinders and 6ft 7in wheels, Nos 400–409, were built in 1916–1921. Some were later rebuilt. Three 5ft 8½in engines were also constructed in 1924–6, Nos 500–502.

447 Especially notable among Irish 4-6-0s were Great Southern Railway Nos 800–802, named after queens of Ireland in Erse lettering, *Maeve*, *Macha*, and *Tailte*. They came out in 1939 and 1940, the last new steam engines to be built for what is now Coras Iompair Eireann. With 6ft 7in wheels, three 18½ × 28in cylinders, and 225lb

447

pressure, they bore an uncanny resemblance to the rebuilt Royal Scots of the LMS (see **451**), although at the time of their appearance only one such engine had appeared. No 800 is preserved in Belfast museum.

448 The 4-6-0 made its debut on the L&YR in 1908 with 20 engines, built by Hughes. Nos 1506–1525 had four 16 × 26in cylinders and 6ft 3in driving wheels. They were not particularly successful machines, but most of them ultimately received superheaters, and were allocated LMS Nos 10400–10419. They were scrapped in the 1920s and 1930s.

More of the class appeared in 1921, of basically the same design, but with modern improvements, and these proved to be quite satisfactory engines. There were initially 35, L&YR Nos 1649–1683, later LMS 10420–10454.

Another 20, which would have been L&YR Nos 1694–1713, came out new as LMS 10455–10474 in 1923–4. These were originally intended to be 4-6-4Ts (see **494**). No 10456 was converted to a four-cylinder compound in 1926, and worked some trials over the L&NW main line between Crewe and Carlisle.

448

The only L&YR 4-6-0s to survive nationalisation were 10442 and 10455, the latter scrapped as BR 50455 in 1951.

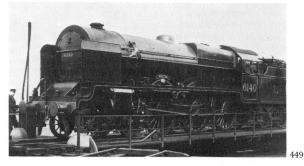

449

449 The first post-grouping 4-6-0s on the LMS were the Royal Scots, 50 engines built straight from the drawing board without any preliminary trials by the North British Locomotive Company in 1927–a modern express passenger engine was urgently needed for the West Coast main line. 20 more followed from Derby works in 1930. The first 25, Nos 6100–6124, were named after famous regiments, as were the Derby-built ones, Nos 6150–6169. Although Nos 6125–6149 started life commemorating names of old locomotives of the earliest period, these also eventually gave way to regimental names. They had three 18 × 26in cylinders, 6ft 9in driving wheels, and 250lb pressure.

An experimental version of the design was built which had a very high pressure boiler with a maximum of no less than 900lb, No 6399 *Fury* (**450**). Unfortunately a

450

451

burst tube during its trials resulted in the death of a travelling inspector on the footplate, and the engine never entered normal service.

Fury was rebuilt by Stanier with a taper boiler in 1935 as No 6170 *British Legion*, in which form it became the prototype to which all of the Royal Scots were eventually converted. (**451**) Their remarkable similarity to the Irish 4-6-0s, with which they had no direct connection, will be very apparent (see **447**).

No 6100 is preserved at Bressingham Hall. This is not the original *Royal Scot*, but No 6152, the number and name being exchanged when the engine went on tour to America in 1933, under the guise of No 6100 *Royal Scot*. These were not restored to their rightful owners when the engine returned.

No 6115 *Scots Guardsman*, withdrawn in 1965, the last to remain in service, is also preserved in working order at the Dinting Railway Centre.

452

452 What came to be known as the Baby Scots, or officially the Patriots comprised in the first place two engines of 1930, which were nominally rebuilds of LNWR Claughtons No 5971 *Patriot* and 5902 *St Dunstan*. 40 more followed, actually new engines although they took the numbers and names of scrapped Claughtons. All of these were later renumbered 5500–5541, and another ten came out in 1934 as 5542–5551.

175

They had 6ft 9in wheels, three 18 × 26in cylinders, and parallel boilers very similar to those on the Royal Scots, to which they were very similar in outline but on a smaller scale. They indicate what a Midland 4-6-0 would have been like if that Company had ever had any. Several were later rebuilt by Stanier with taper boilers, and pressure increased from 200 to 250lb. This made them virtually identical with the rebuilt Royal Scots, and they lasted in this form into the 1960s.

Sir William Stanier, soon after his accession to the post of Chief Mechanical Engineer of LMS, produced two designs of 4-6-0 in 1934. These were the three-cylinder Jubilees for express passenger duties and the even better known Black Fives, general purpose mixed traffic locomotives. As Stanier had come from the Great Western it was not surprising that there was evidence of Swindon in his new engines, notably the domeless taper boiler which was applied to earlier examples of both the new classes. This was found to be not very suitable for the LMS engines, and the later ones were built new with domed boilers.

453 The Jubilees were found to be excellent engines outside the top link range of requirements. They remained the principal express type on the Midland right through to the end of steam working, as well as fully acquitting themselves on other parts of the system. They had 6ft 9in driving wheels and three 17 × 26in cylinders. There were eventually 191 in all, Nos 5552–5742. Nos 5735 and 5736 received larger boilers in 1942 raising the pressure from 225lb to 250lb.

Nos 5593 *Kolhapur*, 5596 *Bahamas*, and 5690 *Leander* have been preserved at various steam centres, the last

453

named in working order, and all restored to LMS maroon livery.

454 Stanier's Black Five, which had 6ft 0in driving wheels, 18½ × 28in cylinders and 225lb pressure soon achieved widespread popularity as being one of the most generally useful engines ever designed, suitable for almost any duty.

They were to be found all over the LMS system from Wick in the far north to Bournemouth in the south, via the S&DJR. There were ultimately no less than 842 of them, beginning with Nos 5000–5471, built between 1934 and 1938; then after a hiatus owing to the war, construction was resumed in 1943 with 5472–5499, 4800–4999, and so on working backwards in batches, eventually completing the range from 44658 upwards, the last ones coming out under BR auspices.

There were sundry variations, mainly in boiler mountings. A few were fitted with double blast pipes and chimney; Nos 44738–44757 had Caprotti valve gear and lower running plates with small splashers (**455**); whilst 44686 and 44687 had no running plates at all, to the great detriment of their looks. No 44767 was unique in having Stephenson's valve gear in place of the normal

Walschaerts (**456**), and this engine is still to be seen on the North Yorkshire Moors Railway as No 4767 under the name *Stephenson*. A number of others still survive at various preservation sites, mostly restored to working order.

454

455

456

457

457 The LMS Black Five was adopted in 1951 by British Railways as one of the 12 standard types for future steam construction, with a few modifications, the most noticeable being the exceptionally high running plate, which had by then become the fashion. 172 had been built by the time the decision to abandon further steam construction had been reached, BR 73000–73171.

458

459

460

Of these 73125–73154 were Caprotti fitted (**458**). No 73129 has been acquired by the Midland Railway Trust at Butterley, Derby, and another of the standard type, No 73050, is on the Nene Valley Railway bearing the name *City of Peterborough*. Another possible candidate for preservation at the time of writing is No 73082 *Camelot*, which was attached to the Southern Region, and inherited the name from an SR King Arthur.

459 BR also produced a lighter version of standard 4-6-0 with 5ft 8in wheels for cross-country and semi-main line work, of which 80 were built between 1951 and 1956, Nos 75000–75079.

No 75027 can be seen at work on the Bluebell Railway, No 75029 on the East Somerset Railway carrying the name *The Green Knight*, and No 75078 on the Keighley & Worth Valley Railway. These last two have double chimneys, which were to be found on some of the class.

4-6-0T

460 The 4-6-0T was a very little used type in the British Isles. Wilson Worsdell built ten such engines for the North Eastern in 1907 for the steeply graded Whitby lines to supersede the 0-4-4Ts then in use. They had two inside cylinders of 19 × 26in and 5ft 1¼in driving wheels. The coal capacity proved insufficient, however, and they were rebuilt as 4-6-2Ts between 1914 and 1917 with enlarged bunkers. In this form they remained at work until 1947–1951, although most of them finished up in the Leeds area.

461 There was one small railway in Ireland which made this rare type its principal class. This was the Cork Bandon and South Coast Railway down in the south west, which became part of the Great Southern Railway at the 1925 amalgamation.

There were nine of them, and they worked most of the main line trains over the long 62 mile route between Cork and Baltimore, regrettably closed entirely in 1961. The first engine was a rebuild of a 4-4-0T of 1892, reconstructed as 4-6-0T in 1906. Another with a larger boiler was built at the same time, with seven more similar ones at intervals up to 1920. The original, which became GSR 471, was scrapped in 1933, but several others lasted until 1961–1965, the end of steam. They had 5ft 2½in wheels and 18 × 24in cylinders.

462 Still in Ireland, 3ft 0in gauge 4-6-0Ts were to be found on the County Donegal, West Clare and Londonderry and Lough Swilly. One of the latter, No 4, was photographed at Londonderry in 1953. It was built in 1902 and bears the initials of the associated Letterkenny & Burtonport Extension Railway which was worked by the L&LSR.

462

461

463

463 There were a number of narrow gauge 4-6-0Ts in England, built by Baldwins in the USA during the First World War, some of which were eventually disposed of to light railways, such as the Ashover, Glyn Valley, and Welsh Highland. These had 2ft 0in driving wheels, 8 × 12in cylinders, and 140lb pressure. Glyn Valley No 4 was photographed at Chirk in 1932. It was acquired in 1921, and scrapped in 1936.

4-6-2

464 The first Pacific in Great Britain was Churchward's *The Great Bear* which saw the light of day on the GWR in 1908. It had four 15 × 26in cylinders, 6ft 8in driving wheels, 228lb pressure and a double bogie tender. In view of its weight it had to be confined to the line between London and Bristol; because of this restricted availability Collett reconstructed it in 1924 as a Castle class 4-6-0. It retained its number 111, but was renamed *Viscount Churchill*.

465 It was not until the last month of the pregrouping era that any further Pacifics appeared, and then almost simultaneously on the GNR and NER. Gresley's design was the well known A1 class, as it was originally known; two engines, Nos 1470 *Great Northern* and 1471 *Sir Frederick Banbury*.

The world famous *Flying Scotsman* followed in February 1923, at first as LNER 1472N, later 4472 as we know it today. Its more recent history is so well known as to be hardly necessary to recapitulate here, sufficient to say that it is the only A3 (as the engines were later reclassified) to have survived, and that it can now often be seen on steam specials over approved BR routes in the north of England.

464

465

466

There were eventually 78 of these engines, which had 6ft 8in driving wheels, three 20 × 26in cylinders, and 180lb pressure, later raised to 220lb. They became BR 60035 to 60113.

The last one was a Thompson rebuild of the original *Great Northern*, the prototype of a new class to be known as A1 which multiplied under Peppercorn to a total of 50 engines, including the original conversion, Nos 60113–60162 (**466**).

Thompson and Peppercorn between them also produced a 6ft 2in version between 1943 and 1948, the first of which were rebuilt from 2-8-2s (see **534**). One of these, restored as LNER 532 *Blue Peter*, can be seen at Dinting Railway Centre.

467

467 The famous A4s, Gresley's streamlined engines built in 1935, caused something of a furore when they came out because of their unconventional appearance. They quickly established themselves as one of the finest designs of express engine ever to be seen in this country. No 4468 *Mallard*, holder of the world speed record for steam of 126½ mph, has earned a well deserved place in York museum. No less than seven others have been preserved, two in America. No 4498 *Sir Nigel Gresley*,

aptly commemorating its designer, is in working order and can sometimes be seen on steam specials.

468 Concurrently with the original Gresley machines, Sir Vincent Raven also introduced his own Pacific for the North Eastern, the first coming out at the end of 1922. There were only five of them, numbered 2400–2404 and classified LNER A2. They were later named after cities, as illustrated by No 2402 *City of York*.

Like the Gresleys, they had three cylinders, 19 × 26in, but driving direct on to the front coupled wheels instead of the centre pair, more usual on six-coupled express engines. This resulted in a very long boiler, giving rise to their nickname of Skittle Alleys. Although potentially very good engines which might have had an interesting future, they had no chance against the obviously superior Gresley machines under the new LNER organisation, and all were scrapped by 1937.

468

469 It was not until Stanier came to the LMS in 1932 that the first Pacific was seen on that railway. The Princess class were certainly impressive engines, sleek and handsome in appearance. Nos 6200 and 6201 came out in 1933 followed by Nos 6203–6212 in 1935. They had four cylinders of 16¼ × 28in, 6ft 6in driving wheels, and 250lb pressure. They soon proved themselves greatly superior to anything previously seen on the LNWR main line. No 6201, on test with a light load of 230 tons, covered the 401½ miles between Euston and Glasgow, non stop, in 353½ minutes. All were withdrawn in 1961–2.

No 6201 *Princess Elizabeth* is preserved at Bulmer's, Hereford, and is sometimes seen on steam specials; No 6203 *Princess Margaret Rose* is with the Midland Railway Trust, Butterley, Derby. Both have been restored to LMS crimson lake livery.

469

No 6202 was an experimental loco derived from the Princess design, having turbine propulsion in place of normal cylinders and reciprocating motion (**470**). After initial teething troubles and various modifications it turned out to be very reliable in service. It was a beautiful engine to see at work, with its soft purr and even torque, resulting in the almost complete absence of slipping even when starting with a heavy load, a fault to which most Pacifics were particularly prone.

470

Whatever advantages it may have possessed however did not justify its retention as an 'odd man out' and in 1952 it was rebuilt with ordinary four cylinder propulsion in line with the others of the class and named *Princess Anne*. Its life under its new metamorphosis was unfortunately only too brief, as it was damaged beyond repair in the disastrous Harrow accident of that year.

471

471 The challenge of Gresley's streamlined Pacifics could not go unanswered and Stanier produced his own version of this revolution in British locomotive appearance – the Coronation class, introduced in 1937. The first engines also received a startling new livery of blue, with horizontal white stripes. The bulbous appearance of these engines seemed to many even more outrageous than Gresley's efforts.

Anyway, later engines of the Duchess class were built to conventional outlines (**472**), to which all of the streamlined ones were eventually modified. The whole series eventually totalled 38 engines, Nos 6220–6257, the last appearing in 1948.

No 6220 on test reached 114 mph in 1937 beating the LNER's 113 mph, a record at that time.

Displaced by diesels on the west coast main line in 1960–1 the class performed relief and standby duties for the next two or three years, until an accountancy edict similar to that relating to the Brighton 2-6-0s (see **364**) decreed that all of the survivors, some 20 in all, several quite recently outshopped, must be taken out of traffic by 31 December 1964. They were to be sorely missed during the next year or two, when failed diesels had to be replaced by nothing larger than a Britannia, and often as not a Black Five, which had to manage as best it could with a full load between Crewe and Carlisle, possibly even without banking assistance over Shap.

No 46235 *City of Birmingham* survives in the Birmingham Museum of Science and Industry. No 6229 *Duchess of Hamilton*, which made a tour of USA between 1939 and 1943 disguised as No 6220 *Coronation*, is in York Museum. 6233 *Duchess of Sutherland* is at Bressingham Hall in working order.

472

473 Pacifics came late and somewhat unexpectedly to the Southern, at a time when it seemed unlikely that that railway with its persistent electrification policy would produce any more express steam locomotives. O. V. Bulleid however, who had been CME since 1937, succeeded in persuading the directors that the day of steam was by no means over, and in spite of the war his first Pacific appeared in June 1941.

The class, which was to total 30 by 1949, had 6ft 2in driving wheels, 18 × 24in cylinders, 250lb pressure, and a number of revolutionary features. They were equipped with a patent valve gear of Bulleid's own design, with a primary drive by means of chains totally enclosed in an oil bath and a thermic syphon, only once before used in Britain. They were streamlined, or airsmoothed, as Bulleid preferred to call it, and he also introduced a new numbering scheme, embodying the wheel classification on the continental principle. The first engine was 21C1, the first two digits representing the number of leading and trailing axles (not wheels, as in the Whyte notation), C signifying three coupled axles and the last digit the running number within the class. Under BR normal numbering was reverted to, 21C1–21C20 becoming

35001–35020 and the last ten built new as 35021–35030. They were named after famous shipping lines and known as the Merchant Navy class.

These engines performed well, and put in a great deal of heavy main line service on the SR to the end of steam. The valve gear was however eventually replaced by conventional Walschaert's gear and the streamlining removed, giving the engines a more orthodox but nevertheless impressive appearance.

No 35028 *Clan Line* is preserved in working order based at Bulmer's, Hereford, and is sometimes seen on main line specials. 35005 *Canadian Pacific* is at Steamtown, Carnforth, and 35029 *Ellerman Lines* is on view at York, partly sectionalised to display the principle of operation.

474 A lightweight version of the Merchant Navies appeared in 1945 commencing with No 21C101. The class eventually totalled 110 engines, 21C101–21C170 and the remainder built new as 34071–34110; the earlier ones becoming 34001–34070. Most bore names appropriate to SR territory, starting with 34001 *Exeter*. Some of the later ones were given names of some of the RAF squadrons which played a part in the defence of the country in the critical early war years; these were known as the Battle of Britain class, although they were in fact no different from the others.

No 34051 commemorated *Sir Winston Churchill* and at the time of writing can be seen at Didcot Railway Centre. Others at preservation centres include 21C123 *Blackmoor Vale*, beautifully repainted in SR malachite green and at work on the Bluebell Railway, 34092 *City of Wells* on the Keighley & Worth Valley, 34039 *Boscastle* on the Main

473

474

Line Steam Trust at Loughborough, and 34016 *Bodmin* on the Mid Hants.

Exactly half of the West Countries were eventually rebuilt and destreamlined (**475**) like the Merchant Navies. They had 6ft 2in driving wheels, 250lb pressure and three $16\frac{3}{8} \times 24$in cylinders. They weighed several tons less than the Merchant Navies, giving them greater route availability such as over the lines west of Exeter, many of which are now closed and known as the 'withered arm' of the SR.

475

476

477

It seems a little strange that the Southern, when already committed to the gradual elimination of steam, should in such a short time, thanks to the efforts of Mr Bulleid who was a self-confessed 'steam dog', accumulate no less than 140 Pacifics. The LMS, with its large network of important main lines, had only 58. The LNER on the other hand had 202 running or planned at the time of nationalisation.

476   The first of the 12 planned British Railways classes to appear in 1951, unlike several of the others which were virtually existing LMS types, was an entirely new design of Pacific in the form of No 70000 *Britannia*. For one thing it had only two cylinders; previous Pacifics in this country had all had either three or four. They came under a certain amount of criticism in their early days, but on the whole acquitted themselves well, especially on the Great Eastern section, which had hitherto seen nothing larger than 4-6-0 on its Norwich expresses.

There were 55 of them in all, Nos 70000–70054, the last five being allocated to Scotland. They had 6ft 2in driving wheels, two 20×28in cylinders, and 250lb pressure.

The original 70000 *Britannia* has been restored to working order and can be seen on the Severn Valley. No 70013 *Oliver Cromwell*, which ran one of the last steam hauled specials in August 1968, went straight to Bressingham Hall, where it is now on exhibition and occasionally steamed.

A lightweight version came out in 1951, Nos 72000–72009, named after Clans for use in Scotland (**477**). Their performance was on the whole indifferent, and although five more were planned for use on the Southern they were never built.

478 No 71000 *Duke of Gloucester* was Riddles' last opportunity to design a large main line express engine for top link duties on the West Coast route. By an irony of fate, it might never have appeared but for the destruction of 46202 in the Harrow Disaster of 1952. This gave an excuse for the building of a replacement locomotive, even though the decision had virtually been made to effect a gradual phasing out of steam, although not quite with the indecent haste with which this was actually put into effect.

No 71000 was a three-cylinder machine with Caprotti valve gear, and might have been the prototype of a long series, but unfortunately it was destined to attain the sad distinction of being the last new express engine in Britain and the only one of its kind.

On withdrawal in 1962 its cylinders and motion were removed for preservation, but the engine itself went to Barry scrapyard, where it languished with inevitable deterioration in its condition. In 1974 a group of enthusiasts purchased it and it was removed to the Great Central Steam Trust at Loughborough. At the time of writing it is undergoing reconstruction, an immense task including the fabrication of new cylinders and valve gear.

478

479

4-6-2T

479 Surprisingly little use has been made of the 4-6-2T, in view of it being such a suitable type for a tank version of the widely popular 4-6-0.

It was first seen almost simultaneously on three railways in 1910. On the North Eastern, 20 engines were built by Sir Vincent Raven for heavy mineral traffic and shunting duties. They had three $16\frac{1}{2} \times 26$in cylinders, with the drive on the leading coupled axles, a normal feature of Raven's engines, and 4ft $7\frac{1}{4}$in driving wheeels. As LNER class A7, they became BR 69770–69789 at the grouping and disappeared during the 1950s.

The NER built no further 4-6-2Ts as such, but acquired two more classes by rebuilding. Class A6 was converted from 4-6-0Ts (see **460**), and class A8 from 4-4-4Ts (see **249**).

480 The first of two very fine 4-6-2Ts came out on the LB&SCR, also in 1910, the work of D. Earle Marsh. The comparatively short main lines of the Brighton made them very well suited to the employment of tank engines; this is a case where, but for this factor, these locomotives might well have been designed as 4-6-0s. Like the 4-4-2T

480

type, the 4-6-2T configuration lent itself well to the design of a well proportioned and handsome locomotive, no better exemplified than in *Abergavenny*, the first of the two, and its sister *Bessborough*, which followed in 1912.

The two 4-6-2Ts were almost identical except that *Bessborough* had Walschaert's valve gear in place of Stephenson's, the principal dimensions being 6ft 7½in driving wheels, 21 × 26in cylinders and a working pressure of 170lb. At the grouping they regrettably lost their names, and became just B325 and B326, later 2325 and 2326, and eventually BR 32325 and 32326.

In their early years they naturally worked on the fast express trains such as those between London and Brighton, but after electrification they gravitated to Tunbridge Wells, the last haven of other express LB&SCR types before them. Both were withdrawn in 1951.

481 The third railway to introduce 4-6-2Ts in 1910 was the LNWR, 47 engines in all, to the design of Bowen Cooke. They had Belpaire fireboxes, the first use of the type on the LNWR. The first ten initially used only saturated steam, with 18½ × 26in inside cylinders; they

were however soon fitted with superheaters and 20 × 26in cylinders, in common with the rest of the class. They had 5ft 8½in driving wheels. Used on outer suburban services from Euston and in the Manchester area, they were also for many years used on the Central Wales line. They became LMS 6950–6996, and the last one was scrapped in 1941.

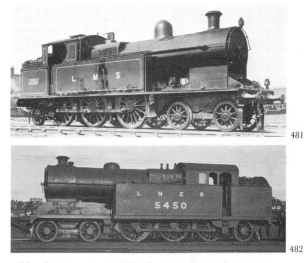

481

482

482 Robinson's 4-6-2Ts for the Great Central were probably the best known of all and undoubtedly rank amongst the finest express tank engines ever built for outer suburban and semi-express work.

Later known as LNER Class A5, 21 were built before the grouping, and another 23 between 1923 and 1926 under Gresley, who was a sufficiently broad-minded man to recognise a good design when he saw one. The later examples were built specifically for use in the North Eastern division.

They had 5ft 7in driving wheels and 20 × 26in inside cylinders. One was destroyed in 1942, but the remaining 43 engines became BR 69800–69842, the last survivor going in 1960. Regrettably only two GCR engines have survived for preservation, and it is a great pity that one of these fine engines, so typical of this period in many ways, did not qualify for this distinction.

483 Pickersgill built 12 4-6-2Ts for the Caledonian in 1917, Nos 944–955, with 5ft 9in driving wheels and 19½ × 26in outside cylinders. They were designed for the semi-express services out of Glasgow to the Ayrshire coast.

Later LMS 15350–15361, some of them survived into BR days. The last in service, in the early 1950s, were to be seen on banking duties up Beattock incline.

484

484 Urie constructed five 4-6-2Ts for the LSWR in 1921. They had 5ft 7in driving wheels and cylinders of 21 × 28in.

As the need for a large suburban passenger tank no longer existed on that railway, for which duty they would have been eminently suitable, they were in fact designed for and used mostly on local freight working, although occasionally on Ascot race specials and other similar occasions. As 30516–30520 they lasted until the early 1960s.

483

485

485 The only 4-6-2Ts in Ireland were eight 3ft 0in gauge engines on the Londonderry & Lough Swilly Railway, built between 1899 and 1910.

4-6-4

486 Only one 4-6-4 tender engine, or Baltic, as they were usually known in the USA, appeared in Britain. This was an experimental locomotive built by Gresley in 1929 at Darlington under conditions of great secrecy. No 10000 had four cylinders coupled with a marine type Yarrow boiler, which had a very high working pressure of 450lb and twin blast pipes. It also had a partly streamlined appearance, the first engine to do so, anticipating the A4s by some five years.

The engine gave a reasonably good account of itself, but was rebuilt in 1937 as a three-cylinder simple, very similar to the A4 streamlined Pacifics, but retaining its 4-6-4 wheel arrangement (**487**). It became BR 60700 and was withdrawn from service in 1959.

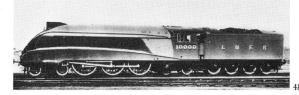

487

4-6-4T

488 The standard gauge 4-6-4T or Baltic tanks made its first appearance in Great Britain in 1912. A number were designed by Mr R. H. Whitelegg for the London Tilbury & Southend Railway, but did not appear until after its absorption by the Midland in that year. They therefore came out as MR 2100 to 2107, in crimson lake livery.

They had two outside cylinders of 20 × 26in with 6ft 3in driving wheels. Although they were intended as

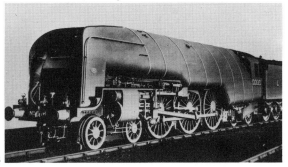

486

488

successors to the very successful 4-4-2Ts on the heaviest trains, they were never very much use on the LT&SR system as their weight prohibited them from working into Fenchurch Street. They spent much of their time on the parent Midland system, for several years being allocated to Wellingborough working double-headed freight trains to Cricklewood (sometimes in combination with a Johnson 4-2-2!), and on local passenger trains out of St Pancras. They were broken up between 1929 and 1934.

489 R. H. Whitelegg became locomotive superintendent of the G&SWR in 1918, and in 1922 built six somewhat similar engines for express services between Glasgow and Ayr. They were incidentally among the very few passenger tank engines ever owned by that railway.

They had 6ft 0in driving wheels and 22 × 26in cylinders. As G&SWR 540–545 they became LMS 15400–15405, but in common with most other engines of that railway they suffered premature extinction, being scrapped in 1935–6.

490 The seven very fine Baltic tanks of the LB&SCR which followed the two 4-6-2Ts of 1910 (see **480**) were the work of L. B. Billinton. Nos 327 and 328 appeared in 1914, followed by Nos 329–333 in 1921–2.

They had 6ft 9in wheels and 22 × 28in cylinders. No 328 was named *Charles C. Macrae*, 329 *Stephenson* (perpetuating both the name and number of the Stroudley 2-2-2 No 329 (see **28**), and 333 became the War Memorial engine *Remembrance*.

The extension of electrification to Eastbourne rendered them largely redundant in their existing form, and

Maunsell rebuilt them in 1934–6 as 4-6-0 tender engines. They were transferred to the Western Section and stationed at Nine Elms, working mainly on the Bournemouth line. Except for *Remembrance* they were named after locomotive engineers of the past, *Stephenson* remaining as it was, the others becoming *Trevithick*, *Hackworth*, *Cudworth*, *Beattie* and *Stroudley*. As BR 32327–32333 they remained in traffic until 1955–7.

489

490

491 In 1920 the Belfast & County Down acquired four engines which were unsuperheated, unusual for such a design at this period. They had outside cylinders, of 19 × 26in, and 5ft 9in driving wheels. Originally BCDR 22–25, they became Ulster Transport Association 222–225 and lasted until dieselisation in 1956.

491

493

494

492

493 On the Furness Railway Mr D. L. Rutherford built five inside-cylinder 4-6-4Ts in 1920, and, like the B&CDR engines, they were unsuperheated. They had 5ft 8in wheels and $19\frac{1}{2} \times 26$in cylinders. As LMS 11100–11104 all went in the mid-1930s except 11103, which lasted until 1940.

492 Other Irish 4-6-4Ts were to be found on the 3ft 0in narrow gauge, actually the earliest engines of the type in the British Isles, having been built for the County Donegal Railway by Nasmyth Wilson in 1904. They had Belpaire fireboxes, unusual for the period, and were later superheated. The cylinders were 15×21in and they had 3ft 9in driving wheels. They were in service until 1953–4.

494 The last 4-6-4Ts to be built actually came out on the LMS after the grouping, although they were a pure L&YR design, a tank version of Hughes' very successful

4-6-0s (see **448**). There were to have been 30 of them, but in the event only ten came out as tanks, the rest being built to the basic design which duly appeared as LMS 10455–10474 concurrently with the 4-6-4Ts, Nos 11110–11119.

Both versions had the same dimensions, apart from weight: 6ft 9in wheels, 16½ × 26in cylinders and 180lb pressure. No 11114 was exhibited at the 1925 Wembley Exhibition. They were found to be too unsteady at speed for express working, for which they had been intended, and too large to be used exclusively on local service, with the result that all were taken out of service between 1938 and 1942.

497

0-8-0

495 The first 0-8-0 tender engines in Great Britain were four built by Sharp Stewart between 1886 and 1888 for a foreign railway but never delivered, which were acquired by the Barry Railway in 1889 and 1897. They were incidentally the only tender engines that railway ever possessed. On absorption by the GWR they became Nos 1387–1390 in that company's list, and they were withdrawn from service between 1927 and 1930, after spending their working lives on local coal trains between the collieries and Barry docks. The tenders, very unusually for the period, had only four wheels.

496 0-8-0s were introduced by F. W. Webb to the LNWR in 1892, initially a two-cylinder simple, followed by a series of four-cylinder compounds, some of which later ran as 2-8-0s (see **524**). All the late survivors were either scrapped or converted to two-cylinder simple 0-8-0s, and in this form the type was perpetuated by Whale and Bowen-Cooke until 1922, by which time there were several hundred of them. They were the LNWR's principal type of heavy freight traffic engine.

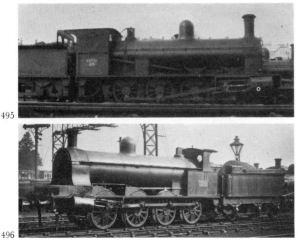
495

496

No 1282, photographed at Nuneaton, was a four-cylinder compound built in 1903, with two outside high-pressure cylinders of 15 × 24in, and two large low-pressure ones of 20½ × 24in housed in the peculiar 'piano front'. This was a distinctive feature of some LNWR engines of the period.

The final superheated development had inside cylinders only (**497**). One of these has been preserved, and can be seen at the Ironbridge Gorge Museum, Telford, Shropshire.

498 The L&YR had 295 engines built between 1900 and 1920 of progressive classes 11 of which were four-cylinder compounds.

498

499

500

501

The final development of the type was a powerful engine with 4ft 6in wheels, 21½ × 26in cylinders and 180lb pressure (**499**). The whole series became LMS No 12700–12994; few lasted until nationalisation, and all had disappeared by 1951.

500 Robinson built 89 0-8-0s, all with two outside cylinders, for the GCR between 1902 and 1910. Withdrawal began before the war, and was completed by 1951. Some were however converted to 0-8-0T shunting engines, and in this form lasted longer (see **513**).

501 Ivatt designed a class of 0-8-0s for the GNR, of which 55 were built between 1901 and 1909. The last of them went in 1937.

502 On the Caledonian, a number of engines were designed on which the second and third axles were set as close together as the 4ft 6in wheels permitted to leave space for the firebox between the third and fourth axles. There were only eight of these somewhat ungainly engines, built between 1901 and 1903, and all had gone by 1929. They became LMS Nos 17990–17997, at that time the highest-numbered engines in Great Britain.

503 The Hull & Barnsley had fifteen 0-8-0s, built in 1907 by The Yorkshire Engine Co. to the design of Matthew Stirling. They had domeless boilers in accord with the tradition of the Stirling family. All were later rebuilt with domes, and taken out of service in 1931.

504 The famous GER Decapod, originally an 0-10-0T (see **542**), ran as an 0-8-0 between 1906 and 1913, with two cylinders in place of the original three. It was employed on freight traffic.

505 The North Eastern, another large user of the 0-8-0 type, had 225 of them, of three classes built from 1901

502

503

504

505

onwards by Wilson Worsdell and Vincent Raven. Most of them had two outside cylinders only, but the last and most powerful class, consisting of 15 engines built between 1919 and 1924 (after the grouping) had three 18½ × 26in cylinders together with 4ft 7½in driving wheels, as did the earlier 0-8-0s.

All of these were withdrawn from service in 1962 and No 63460 (NER 901) was set aside for preservation (**506**). It is now part of the National Railway Museum collection, and at the time of writing is on loan to the North Yorkshire Moors Railway.

507 The final design of 0-8-0 was introduced to the LMS by Sir Henry Fowler in 1929. Very Midland in appearance, these engines could be regarded as what a MR 0-8-0 would have been like if that Company had ever had any. In fact it relied exclusively on 0-6-0s for its freight traffic right through to the end of its independent existence, and never possessed an eight-coupled engine.

175 of the class were built. They had 4ft 8½in wheels, 19½ × 26in cylinders and 200lb pressure. All had gone by 1962.

0-8-0T

508 The earliest 0-8-0Ts in the country – and indeed the first eight-coupled engines of any sort – were two engines built by the Avonside Engineering Company in 1864 for the Vale of Neath Railway (absorbed by the GWR in 1865), and two very similar by the same makers in 1866 for the Great Northern, Nos 472 and 473. These had 4ft 6in wheels and 18½ × 24in cylinders. Both were scrapped in 1880, the Vale of Neath engines having already been withdrawn in 1871 after a very short working life.

506

507

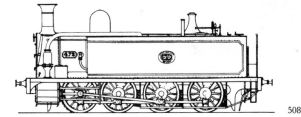

508

509

510

511

509 Following the tender engines (see **502**) McIntosh also built eight 0-8-0Ts for the Caledonian Railway in 1903–4. They had rather longer lives than their tender counterparts, the last one not being withdrawn until 1939.

These two classes were the only eight-coupled engines built for a pregrouping Scottish railway.

510 An 0-8-0ST, a rebuild of an earlier 0-6-2ST for the Wrexham, Mold & Connah's Quay Railway, was taken over by the GCR as No 400. It was scrapped in 1923.

511 An 0-8-0T was built in 1904 for the Kent & East Sussex Railway; it was intended for the projected extension to Maidstone which never materialised. It did little work until 1932, when it was exchanged for an old but much more suitable Beattie 0-6-0ST with the Southern Railway, who gave it the number 949, retaining its name *Hecate*. It shunted in Clapham Junction yard for several years before being scrapped in 1950.

512 In 1929 Mr R. E. L. Maunsell built eight three-cylinder 0-8-0T shunting engines for the SR, Nos A950 to A957. They had 4ft 8in wheels, cylinders of 19 × 26in, and a boiler pressure of 180lb. They weighed 71½ tons. Among other duties such as general shunting, they were also employed as bankers on trains up the 1 in 37 gradient between Exeter St Davids and Queen Street, and one was generally used at Dover marshalling the Wagons Lits sleeping cars on to the Dunkirk ferry boats. All were withdrawn en bloc at the end of 1962.

513 In 1942 it was decided, in view of the shortage of shunting engines for wartime duties, to convert 25 of Robinson's 0-8-0 tender engines (see **500**) to tanks. In the event only 13 were actually converted; these became BR Nos 69925–69937, and all had gone by 1959.

0-8-2T

514 The 0-8-2T, a rare type, was first seen on the Barry Railway in 1896, employed on the heavy short distance coal traffic. Seven engines were built by Sharp Stewart & Co., Nos 79–85. They had two outside cylinders of 20 × 26in and 4ft 5in driving wheels.

Three very similar locomotives came from the same makers in 1901, Nos 17–19, for the Port Talbot Railway, who had already acquired two engines of the same wheel arrangement but of very different design from the Cooke Loco Co., USA, in 1899. These latter had typical American features such as bar frames; they were very much 'Swindonised' in 1908, with taper boilers, and as GWR 1378–9 they were scrapped in 1928–9 (**515**).

Of the others, the Barry engines became GWR 1380–86 and the three later Port Talbot ones 1358–1360 (**516**). All of them were scrapped between 1926 and 1935 except 1358, which managed to last until 1948.

513

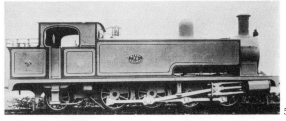

514

512

515

516

517

518

517 When Ivatt introduced his 0-8-2Ts to the GNR in 1903 he intended them for passenger work on suburban trains, including the Metropolitan widened lines.

The 41 engines, GNR Nos 116–156, built up to 1906 differed in detail. The cylinder dimensions varied between 18 and 20 × 26in and there were differences in the size of boiler fitted during their careers; some of them were eventually superheated. They had 4ft 8in driving wheels.

Besides the London area they also worked in the West Riding of Yorkshire and around Nottingham, where most of them eventually finished their days. All were withdrawn between 1927 and 1934.

518 0-8-2Ts were introduced to the LNWR by Bowen Cooke in 1911; these engines had 4ft 5½in driving wheels and 20½ × 24in cylinders. There were 30 of them, built up to 1917. They became LMS 7870–7899, and a few lasted into nationalisation, the last survivor being BR 47877 which went in 1953.

519 The Lancashire & Yorkshire Railway had half a dozen 0-8-2Ts, banking engines built by Hughes in 1908.

519

The last disappeared in 1929. They had 4ft 6in driving wheels and 21½ × 26in cylinders, and were virtually a tank version of his later 0-8-0s. No 1504 and 1505 were photographed at Agecroft in 1927.

0-8-4T

520 An enlarged version of the LNWR 0-8-2T appeared in 1923. Although they came out under the superintendency of H. P. M. Beames they were almost identical with Bowen Cooke's engines, apart from the substitution of a trailing bogie for a pony truck, making them 0-8-4Ts. This resulted in an increase of weight from 72½ tons to 88 tons, and the boiler pressure was raised from 170lb to 185lb. Otherwise their dimensions remained the same.

They were used to a large extent on the Abergavenny – Merthyr line in South Wales with its steep gradients. As they did not appear until after the grouping they carried LMS initials on the side tanks from the start, although the first ones had LNWR numbers. They became LMS 7930–7959 and a few lasted into nationalisation to carry BR numbers between 47930 and 47959.

521 In 1907–8 Robinson on the Great Central built four large 0-8-4Ts for hump shunting in the newly opened yard at Wath-on-Dearne. They had 4ft 8in coupled wheels and three 18 × 26in cylinders. They were numbered 1170–1173, becoming LNER 6170–6173 and were supplemented in 1932 by two further examples, Nos 2798 and 2799.

Although powerful engines they sometimes had difficulty in shunting heavy trains over the humps in slippery weather, and the new ones were consequently fitted with boosters to the trailing bogie, operated by a supplementary power unit with two 10 × 12in cylinders. No 6171 of the original lot was also similarly equipped, and these three received superheaters, as did the remainder in later years. The booster equipment was removed in 1943.

The engines were stationed at Mexborough for use in Wath yard for a good deal of their existence, but two of them worked Whitemoor yard, March, for a time, and also Frodingham. As BR Nos 69900–5 they were made redundant by the coming of the diesel shunter, and were scrapped between 1954 and 1957.

520

521

2-8-0

The 2-8-0, sometimes known as the Consolidation, was destined to become a very important type for heavy goods work on several railways, not to mention its wide military use during both world wars.

522 The first to appear in Britain was Churchward's mineral engine No 97 in 1903. It was in many ways much in advance of its time, and it remained the standard freight design on the Great Western for the rest of the company's existence. It was followed at intervals from 1905 to 1919 by Nos 2801–2883, the original engine becoming 2800. A new series with only slight modifications, Nos 2884–2899 and 3800–3866 followed between 1938 and 1942, by which time Collett had become CME.

All had the standard Churchward 18 × 30in cylinders, with 4ft 7½in wheels. Boiler pressure was 200lb, later increased to 225lb. Superheaters were fitted from 1909 onwards. They were taken out of service during the late 1950s and the 1960s. No 2818 is now in York museum, 2857 at work on the Severn Valley, and 3822 at the Didcot Steam Centre.

523

523 Meanwhile in 1919 Churchward had introduced a 5ft 8in version with a much larger boiler, intended for mixed traffic duties, and indeed they performed a certain amount of passenger work on holiday reliefs. No 4700 was followed by Nos 4701–8 in 1922–3 but no more were built, probably because their weight restricted them to the west of England and Birmingham main lines. They remained in service until the early 1960s.

524 2-8-0s on the LNWR consisted of rebuilds of some of Webb's four-cylinder 0-8-0 compounds of 1901–4 (see **496**), of which 36 were converted around 1906 by the addition of a leading pony truck. Some were also given larger boilers. Several were later reconverted to 0-8-0 simple engines, but some survived the grouping as 2-8-0s being allocated LMS Nos 9600–9615, certain of these again reverting to 0-8-0s.

One of the last to remain in service as a 2-8-0 compound was LNWR No 18, photographed at Willesden in 1924. It was allocated LMS 9602, which it never

522

524

carried before being scrapped in 1928. These were the last of all Webb's notorious compounds to remain in service; possibly the best of a very mixed bag.

525 On the Great Northern, Gresley built 20 two-cylinder 2-8-0s between 1913 and 1919. The first 11 three-cylinder versions appeared in 1919, followed after the grouping by others, until by 1934 there were 67 of them. They had three 18½ × 26in cylinders, 4ft 8in driving wheels and 180lb boiler pressure.

The two-cylinder engines, allocated BR 63475–63494, had all gone by 1952. The three-cylinder variety, BR 63921–63987, with the exception of the first one, all lasted into the 1960s.

526 Although the Midland never had any 2-8-0s in its own right, or any eight-coupled engines at all, for that matter, Fowler did design some for the Somerset & Dorset Joint, for the supply of whose locomotives Derby was responsible. They were of very obvious Midland origin, and consisted of two series, Nos 80–85, built at

Derby in 1914, and Nos 86–90 built by Stephenson & Co. in 1925 with larger boilers, later substituted with smaller ones similar to those of the first series. They had 4ft 8½in driving wheels, 21 × 28in cylinders and 190lb pressure.

They were regularly used on passenger trains during the summer season, over the hilly road of the S&DJR and as BR 53800–53810 they remained in service until 1959–64. Nos 53808 and 53809 have been secured for preservation, the former on the West Somerset Railway, and the latter on the North Yorkshire Moors Railway.

525

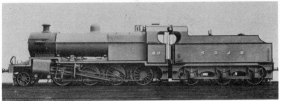

526

527 In 1911 Robinson produced a highly successful design of 2-8-0 for the GCR. They had 4ft 8in driving wheels, 21 × 28in cylinders, and 180lb pressure. Some had larger boilers and there were later several modifications caused by rebuilding.

Apart from the 130 engines built by the GCR for its own use up to 1920, the design was adopted by the Government during the First World War for overseas service, and several hundred were built by outside firms for this purpose. After the cessation of hostilities these were disposed of by the War Department. The LNWR had 30, supplemented by a further 25 in 1927 when it had become part of the LMS; the GWR had 100; and others were loaned to several other railways for a period. The LNER eventually absorbed another 273 into its own stock. Others went to China and Australia.

The class was again brought into use by the Railway Operating Department of the Royal Engineers at the beginning of the Second World War. 92 of the LNER engines were commandeered for use overseas, some of them being the same ones which had done duty in 1917–18. They went mainly to Egypt and Palestine, and never came back.

Of the 100 engines acquired by the GWR in 1919 and 1925, half of them were in service for only a short time, being withdrawn between 1928 and 1930. Most of the remainder lasted until the 1950s.

The LNWR/LMS ones disappeared by 1933. Of those which had come into the hands of the LNER as successors to the line of their origin, many remained in service until the last days of steam in the 1960s.

In 1944 Thompson gave some of them an entirely new look by the substitution of a round topped firebox in

527

528

place of the Belpaire, Walschaert's valve gear and a high running plate clear of the driving wheels. The typical Robinson chimney also gave way to one of GNR design (**528**).

529 When Stanier introduced his class 8F on the LMS in 1935, he provided that railway with something of which it had long been in need, a good heavy mineral engine of sound design. The Midland had never had anything larger than the 0-6-0, which they preferred to use in pairs for their heavy goods trains. Their successors, the LMS 0-8-0s, built in 1929 by Fowler, had never proved satisfactory. The LNWR and L&YR both had excellent studs of efficient 0-8-0s, but the new 2-8-0 quickly established itself as far superior to any of them.

The 8F had 4ft 8½in driving wheels, 18½ × 28in cylinders, and 225lb pressure. The first 12 engines had domeless boilers, but apart from this there were no further modifications to the design of any significance throughout the whole of their careers. To achieve such immediate success straight off the drawing board was rare with such an important design.

Production continued steadily right into the war period, and by 1942 a total of 226 had been built by the LMS purely for its own needs, Nos 8200–8225. Thereafter the story becomes complicated, somewhat akin to that of the GCR Robinson engines just described, and again far too involved to go into in great detail (there are in fact three whole volumes devoted to the complete histories of the WD 2-8-0s of both world wars).

Very briefly, the LMS design was chosen for construction for war needs on a large scale, just as the GCR design had been 25 years earlier. 240 engines were ordered for the War Department in 1939 from three firms, the North British Loco Co., Messrs Beyer Peacock and the Vulcan Foundry. They were allocated WD Nos 300–539. Some of these ran for a time as LMS engines being No 8226 upwards before transfer to WD stock. Later, when the need became greatest in 1942, a number of the original pre-war LMS ones between 8012 and 8094 were commandeered by the WD and sent abroad to the Middle East. Some eventually returned to resume their old identities.

From 1943 onwards many more were built for home use, not all at the LMS works at Crewe or Horwich, but also at Swindon, Doncaster, Darlington, Eastleigh and

529

Brighton. A portent perhaps of things to come with the onset of nationalisation.

The complicated story of this class can best be portrayed by one example, typical of many others, but extremely appropriate in this case. No 8233 was built by the North British Loco Co. in 1940, transferred to the War Department in 1941 as WD 307, and sent overseas to become Iran State No 41.109. Returned to this country as WD 70307 in 1952, it was repaired at Derby as WD 500, returned to stock as BR 48773, withdrawn in 1968 and acquired by the Stanier Loco Society. It now works on the Severn Valley Railway in its original state as LMS 8233. Two others have been preserved; 8431, built at Swindon in 1944, can be seen on the Keighley & Worth Valley Railway; and 48151 is on the Yorkshire Dales Railway.

On British Railways itself, this was one of the last classes to remain in traffic right to the end of steam in 1968.

530 To supplement the use of LMS type 2-8-0s for war needs, Mr R. A. Riddles, then in charge of the War Department and later to become BR's first loco superintendent, designed a new type of 2-8-0 known as the Austerity, of which no less than 939 appeared between 1942 and 1944. They had 4ft 8½in driving wheels, 19 × 28in cylinders, and 225lb pressure.

Many worked in this country on loan to the four railway groups, but others went overseas. Eventually 733 came into the hands of BR as Nos 90000–90732, the last one receiving the name *Vulcan* after the Vulcan Foundry, one of the two firms which had undertaken the construction of this large number of locos.

Although many of them lasted into the 1960s, it was strange that none survived for preservation, and it was left to the Keighley & Worth Valley Railway to reimport one of the last remaining specimens in existence from Sweden. Built in 1945 as WD 79257, it went to Holland, becoming Dutch State Railways 4464. Sold in 1952 to the Swedish State as their No 1931, it was finally rescued and brought back to this country in 1976.

531

531 Although not a British design, and perhaps not quite relevant to these pages, mention should be made of the USA 2-8-0s built for the Second World War, some of which saw brief service in Britain during the war years in transit from the United States to the European theatre of war. They were of course of typical American design with their bar frames and so on.

The enterprising Keighley & Worth Valley Railway has recently secured one of these engines from Poland, photographed here near Haworth in 1978.

2-8-0T

532 The only 2-8-0Ts in this country were on the Great Western, introduced by Churchward for heavy short haul coal trains in South Wales. They had 4ft 7½in driving wheels and 19 × 30in cylinders. Originally 195 engines were built between 1910 and 1930, Nos 4200–4299 and 5200–5294.

Between 1934 and 1939 54 of them were rebuilt as 2-8-2Ts, including 5255–5294, which had been placed in store and never ran in service as 2-8-0Ts. Somewhat curiously, another ten, of a new series, numbered 5255–5264, were built in 1940.

530

532

Nearly all lasted until the 1960s. No 5239 is preserved in working order on the Torbay Steam Railway, and No 5224 is at the Great Central Railway Main Line Trust, Loughborough.

2-8-2

533 Apart from the few GWR 5ft 8in 2-8-0s, the only eight-coupled engines built for passenger work in Great Britain were six 2-8-2s, usually known as Mikados, built by Gresley in 1935–6 for the Edinburgh to Aberdeen route, Nos 2001–2006. No 2001 was *Cock o' the North* and the others also had appropriate Scottish names.

They had three cylinders and 6ft 2in driving wheels, but differed in detail. No 2001 had Lentz poppet valves, and others were semi-streamlined in the A4 style. Their long rigid wheelbase was not found to be too satisfactory and all were rebuilt as 4-6-2s in 1944–5. As BR 60501–60506 they finished their days on the GNR main line until withdrawn between 1959 and 1961.

534 Gresley built two large 2-8-2 mineral engines in 1925 for heavy coal trains between Peterborough and London, Nos 2393 and 2394. They had 5ft 2in driving wheels and three 20 × 26in cylinders, together with a booster to the trailing wheels with two 10 × 12in cylinders. Otherwise they were largely identical with the A3 Pacifics.

They were found to be unnecessarily powerful in that they had short lives, particularly by Irish standards. accommodated on the passing loops of the GNR main line, most of which consisted of only two tracks. They were scrapped in 1945.

533

534

535

536

537

2-8-2T

535 The GWR 2-8-2Ts were all rebuilds of the 2-8-0Ts (see **532**), with larger bunkers to give a wider range of operation. Apart from the increase in weight, amounting to eleven tons, and of course length, the dimensions were the same. They appeared in this rebuilt form between 1934 and 1939 as Nos 7200–7253, most of them lasting nearly to the end of steam working on the Western Region. No 7202 is preserved at the Didcot Railway Centre.

4-8-0

Although the 4-8-0 tender engine was common abroad and had been contemplated on one or two British railways at various periods, the design never got further than the drawing board.

536 It was only on the remote 3ft 0in gauge Irish line of the Londonderry & Lough Swilly Railway that the type was ever seen in the British Isles. There were only two of them, built in 1905 by Hudswell Clarke for working over the long tracks of the associated Letterkenny & Burtonport Extension Railway.

They had 3ft 9in coupled wheels and 15 × 22in cylinders, and were numbered 11 and 12. The first one was scrapped in 1933, but No 12 remained at work until the L&BER was closed in 1947.

4-8-4T

537 It is convenient to take in here the 4-8-4T slightly out of sequence, as it can be readily paired with the L&LSR 4-8-0s. Here again they were unique in being the only examples of their type in Great Britain and Ireland.

Nos 5 and 6, built in 1912, again by Hudswell Clarke, were also intended for the Burtonport extension, but did in fact spend most of their time working between Londonderry and Buncrana on the parent L&LSR system. Like their counterparts, they had 3ft 9in wheels, but the cylinders were 16 × 20in.

They were massive machines for the narrow gauge, weighing 58¾ tons, and would have been large engines even on the standard Irish 5ft 3in gauge. They were not scrapped until 1954 after the final closure of the L&LSR.

4-8-0T

538 The only other eight-coupled engines in Ireland were two 5ft 3in gauge 4-8-0Ts on the Great Southern. Only one engine was built initially, No 900, which appeared in 1914. It had 4ft 6½in driving wheels and 19¼ × 26in cylinders. It was intended for heavy shunting duties in the Dublin yards and banking up to Inchicore. Maunsell had already prepared designs for a three-cylinder 0-8-2T before he left the GS&W in 1913, but this was abandoned by Watson in favour of his own 4-8-0T.

A second engine followed in 1924, by which time it would be thought that any shortcomings in the design would have become apparent. That they were not altogether satisfactory however is shown by the fact that they had short lives, particularly by Irish standards. No 900 was withdrawn in 1929 and No 901 followed in 1931.

539 In 1909 Raven on the NER produced ten three-cylinder 4-8-0Ts for heavy shunting, Nos 1350–1359, and Gresley added another five in 1925, Nos 1656–1660. Two were scrapped in 1937, but the remainder lasted until 1957–61 as BR 69910–69922.

539

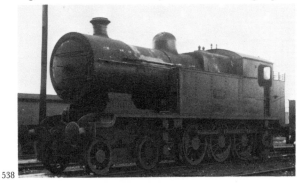
538

540 A third design of 4-8-0T for heavy shunting consisted of four engines built by Urie on the LSWR in 1921, for use in the new hump yard at Feltham. These had 5ft 1in wheels and 22 × 28in cylinders, and weighed 95 tons. They became BR 30492–30495 and worked until 1959–1962.

540

541

0-10-0

541 The only 0-10-0 tender engine in Britain was the famous banker for the Lickey Incline, which appeared from Derby works at the end of 1919. It was the only really large engine ever to be constructed for the Midland Railway, which otherwise had never even used eight-coupled locomotives apart from those built specially for the Somerset & Dorset Joint Railway (see **526**).

The Lickey Banker had four cylinders of 16¾ × 28in with Walschaert's valve gear, 4ft 7½in wheels and 180lb

pressure. Apart from some early trials between Toton and Cricklewood it spent its whole life pounding up the three miles of continuous ascent at 1 in 37 between Bromsgrove and Blackwell, a job otherwise requiring two or even three 0-6-0Ts.

As it was the only one of its kind, there was a spare boiler built at Derby to ensure as short an absence as possible when it had to visit the shops for repairs.

Originally 2290, later LMS 22290, and finally BR 58100, it was in continuous service until 1956.

0-10-0T

542 Britain's first ten-coupled engine was Holden's Decapod for the Great Eastern, built in 1902 as an experiment to decide whether steam haulage was capable of attaining as great a rate of acceleration as electric

542

traction for suburban working. The result was sufficiently satisfactory to ensure that the question of electrification of the GER was postponed for another 40 years.

Unfortunately the attendant necessity of strengthening the track and bridges to take the 80 ton engine was also deferred, and in the event never carried out. Thus, owing to permanent way restrictions this remarkable engine was never able to run in ordinary service on duties which it had shown itself to be quite capable of performing. It was reconstructed in 1906 as 0-8-0 tender engine with two cylinders and used on freight traffic until 1913 (see **504**). In its original form it was the only ten-coupled engine in the country until the building of the MR Lickey banker. As built the engine had three cylinders of 18½ × 24in, 4ft 6in wheels, and 200lb pressure.

2-10-0

543 Concurrently with the numerous 2-8-0s for the War Department (see **530**) Riddles also produced 150 very similar locomotives with ten coupled wheels. Their dimensions were practically identical. They came out

543

between 1943 and 1945, and, like the 2-8-0s, were all built by two firms, the Vulcan Foundry and the North British Loco Co. Two of the 2-10-0s bore commemorative names, one of which, *North British*, was photographed in 1949.

25 of them came into the hands of BR as 90750–90774, all running in service until 1961–2. One engine, originally No 73651, which worked at Longmoor WD Depot where it had been No 600 *Gordon*, is preserved on the Severn Valley Railway.

544

544 Following the WD 2-10-0s, Riddles decided to adopt the wheel arrangement for one of his new standard BR designs. These were perhaps the most successful and outstanding of all the BR engines, and established themselves during their very short lives as remarkable machines. Although designed primarily for freight traffic, they were soon found suitable for relief passenger work, and for a short time worked expresses between Nottingham and Marylebone, on which they were timed on at least one occasion at a speed of 90 mph.

They had two outside cylinders of 20 × 28in, 5ft 0in driving wheels and 250lb pressure. The first one came out from Crewe in 1954, and there were eventually 251 of them, Nos 92000 to 92250. The last to appear, in March 1960 from Swindon, is well known as being the last steam engine to be built for British Railways, and was appropriately named 92220 *Evening Star*. It is now preserved in working order at York.

Two others which have survived are Nos 92203 *Black Prince* on the East Somerset Railway, and 92240 on the Bluebell Railway. The ruthless scrapping of such fine locomotives with many years of useful service in front of them consequent on the indecent haste to eliminate

545

546

steam was a waste of valuable machinery almost without parallel.

No 92250 was fitted with a Giesl ejector to the exhaust, claimed to achieve a remarkable economy in coal consumption (**545**). It was also tried out on a SR Bulleid Pacific. However the authorities were not at this stage really interested in improving the performance of the steam locomotive and the experiments were only carried out in a half-hearted manner. In any case it should have been applied to an older type of locomotive rather than to two classes which already had a high thermal efficiency.

An earlier and much more meaningful experiment with these engines was the building of ten of them, Nos 92020–92029, with Franco Crosti boilers, already tried out with considerable success in Italy (**546**). Briefly this consisted of a small secondary boiler beneath the main one, into which the hot gases were turned back and ejected through a chimney placed alongside the main boiler, the normal chimney on the smokebox being blanked off. The object was to conserve energy which would otherwise pass straight into the atmosphere by using it to pre-heat the water entering the main boiler, a kind of elaboration of the feedwater heaters introduced many years before and used by a number of locomotive designers. The auxiliary boiler was eventually put out of action and the engines reverted to normal exhaust through the smokebox chimney. These engines were not popular with drivers owing to the exhaust from the side chimney obscuring the view from the cab, reviving an old fault which had occurred with many earlier large-boilered engines, and cured only by the fitting of smoke-box deflectors.

MISCELLANEOUS TYPES

Over the years a number of engines have appeared in Britain which have been designed on principles differing from those of the normal steam locomotive. Some of these, conversions of more conventional designs, have been mentioned in the main text, for example Stanier's turbine locomotive (see **470**). Others, however, do not have any place in the sequence hitherto adhered to. These are the articulated locomotives – the Garratt, Fairlie and Mallet types; geared engines, built on traction engine principles; and the steam railcars.

Garratt

The Garratt, a patent design of Messrs Beyer Peacock & Co., was introduced in 1909. It was virtually two engines in one, with a central common boiler and individual articulated driving units at either end. It came to be very popular abroad, particularly on the African continent where it can still be seen, but never caught on to any great extent in Britain where the uses for powerful articulated locomotives are rather limited. There is some diversity of opinion as to whether they should be classified as tank engines, in that they have no separate detachable tender, but their general overall appearance hardly falls within the normal conception of a tank loco.

547 The first Garratt in Britain was a small 0-4-4-0 built in 1924 for a steelworks in South Wales, and a few similar machines were supplied for industrial use.

One of these, used at Baddesley colliery, Warwick, appeared in 1937, the last Garratt to be built for use in

547

this country. It had 3ft 4in driving wheels and 13½ × 20in cylinders, and can now be seen at Bressingham Hall.

The original Garratt of 1909, built for the two foot gauge Tasmanian Government Railway, was re-imported to this country in 1947 and is now in York Museum.

548 So far as the main lines are concerned, Gresley had a solitary specimen built for the LNER in 1925 for

548

banking duties on the Worsborough incline, near Barnsley. This 2-8-8-2 was and remained the largest and most powerful steam engine ever seen in the British Isles, the equivalent of a couple of 2-8-0s. The two independent power units each had three 18½ × 26in cylinders and 4ft 8in driving wheels; pressure was 180lb, tractive effort 72940lb and weight 178 tons. Originally LNER 2395, later 9999, it became BR 69999 and was in service until 1955. It spent its last few years on the Lickey incline in company with the Midland 0-10-0 (see **541**).

549   The only other main line railway to use the Garratt was the LMS. They were rather smaller 2-6-6-2s, and three engines appeared initially in 1927, Nos 4997–4999, to be followed by another 30, Nos 4967–4996. They were employed on coal trains between Toton and Cricklewood, and were successful in going some way to eliminating the practice of double-heading inherited from the Midland; there were never enough of them however to achieve this to any considerable extent.

To ease the onerous task of firing such a large engine they were nearly all fitted in later years with revolving bunkers. They had two sets of 18½ × 26in cylinders, 5ft 3in driving wheels, 190lb pressure, 45620lb tractive effort, and weighed 155½ tons. As BR 47967–47999 they were scrapped in the later 1950s.

Fairlie

During the 1850s Robert Fairlie experimented with locomotives in which the driving wheels, instead of being rigidly attached to the frames, formed an independent power bogie giving greater flexibility on curves. Two 0-4-4Ts on this principle were used on the GS&WR with some success, and one was to be found on the Swindon,

Marlborough and Andover Junction Railway (see **97**). In the 1860s he produced the logical development of this idea, with two driven power units supporting a single rigid frame. On this were mounted two boilers with a central firebox position and a chimney at each end. As with the Garratt, the arrangement was more popular overseas, especially in South America, but representatives of the type are still to be found in Britain.

549

550

550   The narrow gauge Festiniog Railway acquired four 0-4-4-0Ts between 1869 and 1885, two of them built

551

552

at its own works at Portmadoc, and they fully lived up to the maker's claims by handling very long trains with ease.

Two survived until the railway's closure in 1946, and are now to be found at work on what was one of the first of many preserved railways. The driving wheels are 3ft 9in with four cylinders of 9 × 14in and a working pressure of 160lb (**551**).

One of these original engines was replaced in 1979 by the construction of an entirely new one by the FR at its works at Portmadoc, almost exactly to the existing design.

Mallet

552 Engines on a similar principle, but with a single boiler, to the patent of M. Mallet were found on many European railways. The only example in this country was a solitary 0-4-4-0T built by Bagnall of Stafford in 1953 for the 2ft 6in gauge industrial railway operated by Bowater's Paper Mills at Sittingbourne. It was acquired in 1966 by the Welshpool & Llanfair Preservation Society.

Steam Railcar

During the earlier years of the century, between 1903 and 1911 to be precise, many railways attempted to reduce operational costs on branch lines where traffic was of a low density by the use of a single saloon coach embodying a small engine unit. This was usually an 0-4-0T forming the bogie at one end of the vehicle, sometimes completely enclosed within the coach body. The body was in some designs detachable from the locomotive by a pivot. To avoid the need for turning, the railcar could be driven in either direction; a driving cab at the other end of the coach was fitted with certain duplicate controls and a bell code system with which the driver could communicate with the fireman.

553 Drummond on the LSWR built a series of ten engines, 2-2-0Ts, which were entirely independent, working with a saloon trailer. These little engines had 10 × 14in cylinders and 3ft 0in wheels (the average dimensions of this type of railcar). Three of the LSWR engines were ultimately converted to 0-4-0Ts for shunting purposes, and lasted into BR days.

553

554

554 Many of the major railways in Great Britain and some in Ireland employed railcars. By far the largest user was the GWR, with 99 cars, all of the completely enclosed type.

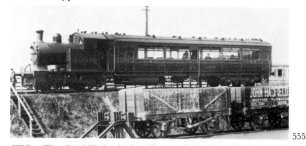

555

555 The L&YR had 18 railcars of the detachable kind. One of these was at work on the Horwich branch until 1948, the last steam railcar to run in the British Isles. Regrettably there are no specimens of these unique examples of the Edwardian travel age still in existence in this country.

Gear- or Chain-driven Railcars and Engines

The Sentinel waggon works of Shrewsbury, which had been constructing Sentinel steam engines since 1906, principally in the form of road vehicles, turned its attention to rail traction in 1923, in the shape of both small shunting engines and railcars for branch line passenger traffic. The main principles of Sentinel design lay in the use of a high pressure boiler with chain or geared transmission to the wheels. The chief user in Britain was the LNER.

556

557

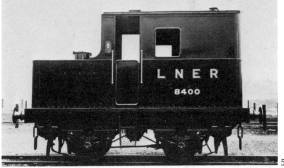

558

556 The first Sentinel-Cammell two-cylinder rail-cars, which were chain driven, appeared in 1925. An improved gear driven version with six cylinders of 6 × 7in, 3ft 1in driving wheels and a 300lb pressure boiler came out in 1928, of which 50 examples appeared up to the year 1931. Five more powerful ones with twin engines were built in 1930–2. All of these engines except the original 1925 ones had names commemorating famous stage coaches of the past.

Although the LNER was the main user the LMS also had 14 similar units. Many of these steam railcars survived the Second World War, one or two as late as 1948, but unfortunately, as in the case of the steam railcars with orthodox engines, there is no example still in existence to represent this important phase of branch line operation.

557 Another firm, Claytons of Lincoln, produced somewhat similar steam railcars in the late 1920s, but only the LNER and the Great Southern Railway in Ireland used them, and they were very short-lived.

558 The first Sentinel shunting engine appeared in 1925, again on the LNER, in the shape of a small 100 HP four-wheeled loco with 2ft 6in wheels, 6¾ × 9in cylinders, and 275lb pressure. It was acquired for use at Lowestoft Harbour.

This engine had only a single speed gearbox, but an improved version appeared in 1921 with two speeds. The number had multiplied to a total of 56 by 1931 (**559**).

Some very similar ones were built for the LMS (**560**) and there were also two of a larger design built for the Somerset & Dorset Railway in 1929 (**561**). The GWR also had a couple. In 1930 the LNER obtained two more of a special design for the Wisbech & Upwell Tramway, with driving cabs at either end for safer working alongside the public road. These had 3ft 2in wheels, four $6\frac{3}{4} \times 9$in cylinders (as against two in the earlier locos), and 275lb pressure (**562**).

Most of these shunters lasted into BR days, a few as late as the 1960s, and one can still be seen at work on the Middleton Railway, Leeds. Sentinel shunters were also used to a considerable extent by various industrial firms, a good example being No 7 of Messrs Ind Coope & Alsop of Burton-on-Trent (**563**).

This was the last design of Sentinel steam shunting loco, production of which ceased in 1957, and several of this type have been acquired by various preservation centres around the country.

559

560

561

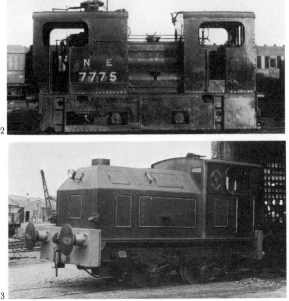

564

564 His 0-6-6-0 Leader class locomotive did not actually appear until after nationalisation, and nothing quite so revolutionary had been seen since the Midland Paget engine of 1908 (see **387**). Its two six-wheeled power units were each driven by a three-cylinder engine with chain transmission in place of coupling rods. The boiler was offset to one side, with a central firebox alongside which the unfortunate fireman had to work in almost impossible conditions, which would hardly be tolerated in these days. In this respect it would probably have been better if the engine had been oil fired.

It was planned to build five of these locomotives but only three, Nos 36001–3, were actually completed and only the first one ever steamed. After a few desultory trials the powers-that-be seemed to lose interest and all three were quietly broken up after a very brief existence.

As would be expected with such an unorthodox engine there were many problems, but none which might not

Bulleid's Articulated Locomotives

Articulated engines, such as Garratts and Fairlies, were rare in the British Isles, but O. V. Bulleid's efforts to prolong the life of steam traction, to which he was such a great adherent, can form a fitting close to this outline of the British steam locomotive.

have been overcome given the will. Unfortunately Bulleid was no longer there to provide the necessary impetus. Had this project been pursued with enthusiasm the engines might have been proved to be a major advance in the use of steam motive power, perhaps going some way towards stemming the tide of dieselisation. It must now be regarded as a last abortive effort to prolong the life of the steam railway locomotive in Britain.

The Leader had 5ft 1in driving wheels, six 12¼ × 15in cylinders, and a boiler pressure of 280lb.

565 After his enforced retirement from BR owing to redundancy caused by nationalisation, Bulleid migrated to Coras Iompair Eireann in Ireland. His opportunities there were unfortunately very limited, as the prospect of dieselisation was already more than a cloud in the sky, and indeed there was far more justification than in the case of Great Britain with its enormous resources of natural coal supplies. Bulleid however was just able to

have his final fling in the construction of his turf burning engine, another articulated 0-6-6-0 very similar in appearance to his abortive SR Leaders.

With no deposits of coal of any economically workable extent, the use of Ireland's only native source of fuel had long been thought of, but never applied with any success to a mobile locomotive, largely owing to its bulk. Nevertheless under Bulleid's direction, after some preliminary experiments with an existing engine, a 2-6-0 (see **371**) he produced his double bogie CC1 (still adhering to his own individual ideas of numbering as referred to in connection with his SR Pacifics).

It had four cylinders of 12 × 14in, 3ft 7in coupled wheels, and a boiler pressure of 250lb. Its estimated weight was 94 tons empty, 118 tons filled. It commenced trials in August 1957. Regrettably the story of his Leader class was repeated – lack of interest – and with Mr Bulleid's retirement in May 1958 the engine languished until 1965, when it too faded into obscurity.

565

Railways owning their own locomotives at the 1923 grouping

London Midland & Scottish Railway

London & North Western
Lancashire & Yorkshire
  These two railways had already amalgamated in 1921.
North London
  Worked by the LNWR from 1909 onwards, but most locos not renumbered into LNWR stock until 1922.
Midland
  Including the London Tilbury & Southend, absorbed by the Midland in 1912; and the Midland (Northern Counties Committee), formerly Belfast & Northern Counties, and including some narrow gauge lines, absorbed by the Midland in 1903. After nationalisation in 1948, BR interests in Northern Ireland were disposed of by the sale of the remains of the former NCC system in 1950 to the Ulster Transport Authority.
Caledonian
Glasgow & South Western
Highland
North Stafford
  Including the Leek & Manifold Valley narrow gauge railway
Furness
Cleator & Workington
Maryport & Carlisle
Garstang & Knott End
Wirral
Stratford on Avon & Midland Junction

London & North Eastern Railway

North Eastern
Hull & Barnsley
  Absorbed by the North Eastern in 1922.
Great Northern
East & West Yorkshire Union
Great Central
  Until 1897 known as the Manchester Sheffield & Lincolnshire.
Lancashire Derbyshire & East Coast
  Absorbed by the GCR in 1907.
Wrexham Mold and Connah's Quay
  Absorbed by the GCR in 1905.
Great Eastern
Colne Valley & Halstead
Mid Suffolk Light
North British
Great North of Scotland

Great Western Railway

Great Western
Liskeard & Looe
  Absorbed by GWR in 1909.
Cambrian
Vale of Rheidol
  Narrow gauge; worked by the Cambrian prior to the grouping, and now the only steam-operated line run by BR.
Welshpool & Llanfair
  Narrow gauge; worked by the Cambrian prior to the grouping.

Mawddwy
  Worked by the Cambrian prior to the grouping.
Midland & South Western Junction
Taff Vale
Barry
Rhymney
Alexandra (Newport & South Wales) docks and railway
Cardiff
Port Talbot railway and docks
South Wales Mineral
  Worked by Port Talbot from 1908 to 1923.
Brecon & Merthyr
Neath & Brecon
Rhondda & Swansea Bay
Burry Port & Gwendraeth Valley
Llanelly & Mynydd Mawr
Gwendraeth Valley
Cleobury Mortimer & Ditton Priors

Southern Railway

London & South Western
Plymouth Devonport & South Western Junction
Lynton & Barnstaple
  Narrow gauge
South Eastern & Chatham
  Formed in 1899 by the amalgamation of South Eastern
  and London Chatham & Dover.
London Brighton & South Coast
Isle of Wight
Isle of Wight Central
Freshwater Yarmouth & Newport

Joint lines owning their own locomotives

Midland & Great Northern Joint
  Owned by the LMS and LNER; locos taken over by
  LNER in 1937.
Somerset & Dorset Joint
  Owned by LMS and SR; locos taken over by LMS in
  1930.

All main line railways were nationalised on January 1 1948 and incorporated into one unit – 'British Railways'. The locomotives were renumbered into a single series by the addition of 40000 to those of the LMS, (with a few exceptions), 60000 to those of the LNER and 30000 to those of the SR. The numbering of GWR engines remained as it was.

Steam locomotive designers

Usually known as Locomotive Superintendents or Chief Mechanical Engineers (referred to as CME in the text). Several changed from one railway to another, as can be seen from the table:

Adams, William	NLR 1853–73
	GER 1873–8
	LSW 1878–95
Adams, J. H.	NSR 1902–15
Allan, Alexander	LNW (Northern Division based on Crewe) 1846–1853
Armstrong, Joseph	GWR 1864–77
Aspinall, Sir John A. F.	GS&W (Ireland) 1883–6
	L&Y 1886–99
Barton-Wright, W.	L&Y 1876–86
Beames, H. P. M.	LNW 1920–3
Beattie, Joseph	LSW 1850–71
Beattie, W. G.	LSW 1871–8
Billinton, L. B.	LBSC 1911–22
Billinton, R. J.	LBSC 1890–1904
Bond, R. C.	BR 1953–8
Bowen-Cooke, C. J.	LNWR 1908–20
Bromley, M.	GER 1878–81
Bulleid, O. V.	SR and BR 1937–49
	CIE (Ireland) 1949–58
Cameron, J.	TVR 1911–22
Churchward, G. J.	GWR 1902–22
Clifford, C.	GNR (I) 1885–1924
Coey, R.	GS&WR 1896–1911
Collett, C. B.	GWR 1922–41
Connor, Benjamin	CR 1856–76
Cowan, W.	GNoS 1857–83
Craven, J. C.	LBSC 1847–69
Cubitt, B.	SER to 1845
	LC&D 1845–60
Cudworth, J.	SER 1845–76
Cumming, C.	HR 1915–23
Cusack, E.	M&GW 1901–15
Dean, William	GWR 1877–1902
Deeley, R. M.	MR 1903–9
Drummond, Dugald	NBR 1875–82
	CR 1882–90
	LSW 1895–1912
Drummond, Peter	HR 1896–1911
	G&SW 1912–18
Fairburn, C. E.	LMS 1944–5
Fletcher, E.	NER 1854–83
Fowler, Sir Henry	MR 1909–23
	LMS 1925–31
Glover, G. T.	GNR(I) 1911–23
Gooch, D.	GWR 1837–64
Gooch, J. V.	LSWR 1841–50
Gresley, Sir Nigel	GNR 1911–22
	LNER 1923–41
Harty, A. W.	GSR (Ireland) 1932–7
Hawksworth, F. W.	GWR 1941–7
Heywood, T.	GNoS 1914–22
Hill, A. J.	GER 1912–22
Holden, J.	GER 1885–1907
Holden, S. D.	GER 1908–12
Holmes, Matthew	NBR 1882–1903

Hookham, J. A.	NSR 1915–23
Hoy, H. A.	L&Y 1899–1904
Hughes, G.	L&Y 1904–22
	LNW 1922
	LMS 1923–5
Ivatt, H. A.	GS&W (Ireland) 1886–96
	GNR 1896–1911
Ivatt, H. G.	LMS 1945–7
Johnson, J.	GNoS 1890–4
Johnson, S. W.	GER 1866–73
	MR 1873–1903
Jones, David	HR 1869–96
Jones, H.	Cambrian 1899–1918
Kirtley, Matthew	MR 1844–73
Kirtley, William	LC&D 1874–99
Lambie, J.	CR 1890–5
Longbottom, L.	NSR 1882–1902
Malcolm, Bowman	Belfast & Northern Counties, MR, NCC 1876–1922 (Longest continuous record as loco superintendent on any railway)
Manson, James	GNoSR 1884–90
	G&SW 1890–1912
Marsh, D. Earle	LBSC 1905–11
Martley, W.	LC&D 1860–74
Maunsell, R. E. L.	GS&W (Ireland) 1911–3
	SE&C 1913–22
	SR 1923–37

McConnell, J. E.	LNW (Southern Division, based on Wolverton) 1846–62
McDonnell, A.	GS&W (Ireland) 1864–83
	NER 1883–4
McIntosh, H.	GNR (Ireland) 1939–50
McIntosh, J. F.	CR 1895–1914
Morton, W. H.	MGW (Ireland) 1915–25
	GSR 1929–32
Park, James Carter	NLR 1873–93
Park, James Crawford	GNR(I) 1880–95
Parker, J.	MS&L 1886–93
Patrick, M.	NCC 1933–46
Peppercorn, A. H.	LNER 1946–7
Pettigrew, W. F.	FR 1897–1918
Pickersgill, W.	GNoS 1894–1914
	CR 1914–23
Pollitt, H.	MS&L and GCR 1893–1900
Pryce, H. J.	NLR 1893–1908
Ramsbottom, J.	LNW (North Eastern Division, based on Manchester) 1857–71
Raven, Sir Vincent	NER 1910–22
Reid, W. P.	NBR 1903–19
Riches, C. T. Hurry	Rhymney 1906–22
Riches, T. Hurry	TVR 1885–1910
Riddles, R. A.	War Dept 1941–3
	BR 1948–53
Robinson, J. G.	GCR 1900–22
Rutherford, D. L.	FR 1918–23
Sacré, C.	MS&L 1859–86
Sinclair, R.	CR 1847–56
	GER 1862–6

Smellie, Hugh	M&C 1870–6
	G&SW 1877–90
Smith, F. G.	HR 1912–15
Stanier, Sir W.	LMS 1932–44
Stirling, James	G&SW 1866–77
	SER 1877–98
Stirling, Matthew	H&B 1885–1922
Stirling, Patrick	G&SW 1853–66
	GNR 1866–95
Stroudley, W.	HR 1866–9
	LBSC 1870–89
Sturrock, A.	GNR 1850–66
Thompson, E.	LNER 1941–6
Trevithick, F.	LNW (Northern Division based on Crewe) 1846–57
Urie, R. W.	LSW 1912–22
Wainwright, H. S.	SE&C 1899–1913
Wallace, W. K.	NCC 1922–30
Watson, E. A.	GS&W (Ireland) 1913–25
Webb, F. W.	LNW 1871–1903
Whale, G.	LNW 1903–8
Wheatley, T.	NBR 1867–74
Whitelegg, R. H.	LT&S 1910–12
	G&SW 1918–23
Whitelegg, T.	LT&S 1880–1910
Worsdell, T. W.	GER 1881–5
	NER 1885–90
Worsdell, Wilson	NER 1890–1910

INDEX